Sun:
The Supreme Creator

Sun:
The Supreme Creator

A Research Work on Astrological Aspects of the Sun

Author

Ajay Srivastava

Jyotirvid, Jyotirvisharad

First Edition, 2025

Published by:

Ajay Kumar Srivastava

45, Awas Vikas Colony, Betiya Hata,

Gorakhpur – 273001 (U.P.), India

Mobile No.: +91-9867837184

Lord Sun

Prayer

ॐ भास्कराय विद्महे मार्त्तण्डाय धीमहि तन्नः सूर्यः प्रचोदयात् ।।

‖ Om Bhaskaray Vidmahe Martanday Dheemahi Tanah
Surya Prachodayat ‖

(**Translation:** Let me meditate on the Sun God, the maker of the day. Let the Sun God grant me higher intellect and illuminate my mind.)

Dedication

I dedicate this book to my father (Late) Sri R.A.L Srivastava who taught me to be an independent, courageous and determined person, and my mother Maya Srivastava whose unconditional love and support always help me to overcome all the obstacles in my life. She has a selfless spirit and served others throughout her life. Her immense patience is peerless and she always inspires me to go ahead.

Preface

Ever since I started learning astrology, I have closely studied the astrological aspects related to the Sun of many human beings and their activities. I found that the position of the Sun in a particular house (bhav) decides the final decision taken by the individual, as the Sun represents the soul and every soul has some purpose for their birth. Every action done by a person strengthens his soul's purpose. Giving is a noble act and selfless giving is essential to strengthen the soul.

The rules of life are reversed, here the giver benefits and the one who snatches suffers loss. Sun is the supreme creator of the universe who teaches us to give. The one who gives is the one who gets stronger; the one who gives is the one who grows; the one who gives is the one who can create.

But people are stingy and think a hundred times before giving and give only what is useless or when they see their own profit. Donation is given in the temple only when there is certainty of getting benefit from God, when it is certain then there is no hesitation in giving but it has no meaning.

This is not charity, this is business and there is no business on the path of God. But people do business in the name of God and create fear in giving charity. It is pure business where both the giver and the taker are looking for assurance of profits. What is given selflessly becomes wealth in the path of God. That is the real wealth and the biggest sacrifice is the sacrifice of ego. Man gives up everything but preserves his ego, hence Sun symbolizes self-awareness, one's core identity and ego and renunciation of ego represents purity; hence, Sun represents Sattva (goodness).

When a person develops the quality of giving and the quality of renouncing his ego, then the quality of goodness starts developing in him and having that quality, the person never snatches anything from others. Hence, Sun never snatches anything and Rahu never gives. The power of Sun increases by giving and the power of Rahu increases by snatching. Sunlight shows people the right path and Rahu's illusion misleads people from the right path. Giving and taking are two different actions and both cannot happen simultaneously, these energies work opposite to each other. Hence, both Sun and Rahu are opposite to each other. Therefore, light begins to be born within the giver, he moves forward on the path of God and the snatcher starts wandering in darkness. Therefore, in Hindu culture we donate after the eclipse because the Sun has become weak due to the eclipse and it is necessary to strengthen it.

The One who is giving without any desire, the One who is giving energy to all the planets, due to which life on earth is energetic and has been going on smoothly for centuries. With His blessing's darkness removes and the person is able to see the light. I obey and bow down Lord Sun, it is only by His grace that I have been able to complete this book.

I give special thanks to my younger brother Abhay Srivastava for their valuable suggestions, without which such work would not have been possible.

I thank God for completing this book. It is not possible for me to write my thoughts into words without the grace of the "Almighty".

Ajay Srivastava

November 11, 2023

Navi Mumbai

Acknowledgement

The existence of this book would not have been possible without the help of my wife Seema and my daughter Saanvi. They provided me enough help to write down my thoughts which I have collected so far in my life. My wife has been instrumental as an illustrator and proof-reader and has given me enough insights to write the matter in a simple and explanatory manner.

Ajay Srivastava

Contents

Chapter 1

Introduction

The seven horses of the Sun represent the seven colors which are the seven chakras of our body. Sun symbolizes the soul and our soul is connected to these seven chakras and these chakras are in constant motion.

It is said in ancient texts that Lord Sun always roams around riding on his seven horses. This tells that due to the rotation of the Sun, there is continuous movement in the seven chakras of our body and life remains dynamic on the earth. As soon as the soul leaves the body, the movement of these chakras ends and the body dies.

When the Sun rises in the morning, activities begin in the world. It is the Sun that leads the activities of the entire day. During the afternoon the Sun is very bright and the activities in the world are fast and people run here and there to fulfill their responsibilities. As the Sun goes below the horizon the activities start slowing down and at night people go to their beds. It is the Sun who controls everything.

We survive on Earth due to the rotation of the Sun. According to astrology, as long as the Sun continues to rotate, life will continue on Earth. As soon as the Sun's rotation ends, every movement will stop and life will end. Because every soul is connected to the Sun, it comes from the Sun and after death it merges into the Sun.

As long as there is any trace of darkness left in the soul, it has to come back on earth and darkness is Rahu. Hence, without complete elimination of Rahu, light cannot be seen. Therefore, both darkness and light (Sun and Rahu) are enemies of each other and can never exist together. When the Sun sets in the evening, activities related to Rahu start taking shape.

• Rahu is temptation

• Rahu is thief

• Rahu represents conspiracy

• Rahu is criminal, and criminal activities take shape in the darkness

Rahu do every act against the Sun. Therefore, a person who is looking for light should stop all kind of association with Rahu only then his journey towards light begins.

The fully illuminated soul never returns because there is no darkness left. Man's life is a journey from darkness to light. It is a search for light in utter darkness where even after years of trying, not even a ray of light is visible, yet the search continues, the ray of hope remains alive and the search continues for births.

When a man clearly refuses to cooperate in any action of Rahu, he does not tie new karmic chains and cuts the old chains one by one. This human life is a search for light, and the darkness starts going away from the life of the one who searches, and such a person moves forward on the path of light. Hence, the ancient sages have sung in the Upanishads;

ॐ असतो मा सद्गमय।
तमसो मा ज्योतिर्गमय ।
मृत्योर्मा अमृतं गमय।

Translation: O Lord, lead me from untruth to truth. Lead me from darkness to light. Take me from death to immortality.

Chapter 2

Astronomy

The Sun is the center of our solar system. Its gravity holds the Solar System together, keeping everything from the largest planets to the smallest pieces of debris in orbit around it. It is the only star in our solar system and has an 11-year cycle of magnetic activity called sunspots.

The Sun is Earth's primary source of light and heat, however, Earth receives only one billionth of the total energy produced by the Sun. It has an extremely important impact on our planet: it drives weather, ocean currents, seasons and climate, and makes plant life possible through photosynthesis. Without the sun's heat and light, life would not exist on Earth. Light takes about eight minutes and 19 seconds to reach Earth from the Sun.

Namesake: The Sun has been called by many names. The Latin word for Sun is "sol"; In Greek and Roman mythology, Apollo is the god of the Sun. In India, Sun is worshiped as Surya God.

Composition: The Sun is not a solid mass; it is made up of a fiery combination of gases. These gases are in the form of plasma. About three-quarters of the Sun is hydrogen, which is constantly fusing together to form helium by a process called nuclear fusion.

Temperature: The temperature of the surface of the Sun is so high that no solid or liquid can exist there; as a result, there is no fixed surface. The surface of the Sun is about 10,000 degrees Fahrenheit (5,500 degrees Celsius) hot, while temperatures in the core reach more than 27 million F (15 million C).

Mass: Its mass is 333,000 times that of Earth, and comprises about 99.8 percent of the mass of the entire Solar System.

Distance from Earth: The Sun is approximately 150 million kilometers (93 million miles) away from Earth.

Rotation: The Sun rotates on its axis just like the Earth. It rotates in an anti-clockwise direction and takes 25 to 35 days to complete one rotation.

Electromagnetic Radiation: The Sun's energy reaches Earth at the speed of light in the form of electromagnetic radiation (EMR). Most electromagnetic waves coming from the Sun are invisible to us. The most high-frequency waves emitted by the Sun are gamma rays, X-rays, and ultraviolet radiation (UV rays). The most harmful UV rays are almost completely absorbed by the Earth's atmosphere; less powerful UV rays circulate in the atmosphere, and can cause sunburn.

The Sun also emits infrared radiation – whose waves have very low frequency. Most of the heat from the Sun comes in the form of infrared energy. Between infrared and UV lies the visible spectrum, which includes all the colors we can see. Red has the longest wavelength (closest to infrared), and violet (closest to UV) the shortest.

Color: The Sun itself is white, meaning it contains all the colors of the visible spectrum. The Sun appears orange-yellow because the blue light it emits has a shorter wavelength, and it is scattered in the atmosphere – the same process that makes the sky appear blue.

Chapter 3

Sun in Astrology

Sun is a fiery, dry, and masculine planet. It is a sattvic planet and controls our consciousness. It is the source of life and light on earth and rules ancestors. It signifies good health, vitality and wellbeing. It represents coarse clothes and the age of 50 years old. It represents the summer season and organic matter. It represents bones, average height, steadfast tendency, and upward direction.

The position of the Sun in the horoscope indicates that the light of the Sun exist in that house and the person can't hide any matter related to that house. For example, if Sun is placed in 10th house and the person involve in doing illegal activities then one day all his activities will be known to everyone and the person himself is responsible for all the consequences.

Appearance: Sun is the God who has four hands which contain lotus, conch, chakra and mace.

Direction and Digbala: The direction of the Sun is east. It gets directional strength (Digbala) in the 10th house and weakness when it is placed in the 4th house.

Natural Karaka: Sun is the natural karaka of 1st house.

Nakshatras Owned by the Sun: Krittika, Uttara Phalguni, and Uttara Ashadha. Whenever the Sun transits in these nakshatras, it enhances the prospects of the planet located in it.

Colour: Red

Caste: Kshatriya

Metal: Gold and Copper

Gemstone: Ruby

Friendly Planet: Moon, Mars, Jupiter

Neutral Planet: Mercury

Enemy Planet: Venus, Saturn, Rahu, Ketu

Aspect: The Sun, from its position, full aspects the seventh house.

Places: It represents temples, places of worship and mountain trees.

Taste: It represents pungent taste like; onion, ginger, black pepper, chilies, etc.

Body parts: Sun rules our head, brain, eyes, heart, lungs, blood, and circulation.

Finger: The ring finger is connected to the Sun.

Diseases: Blood pressure, eye diseases, fever, cerebral disorders, etc.

Affliction: If the Sun is afflicted in the horoscope, then the person will easily become tempered, arrogant, jealous, irritable, dominating, pretentious, lavish, conceit, and haughty. The person can suffer from low stamina and indecisiveness. Baldness, weak eyesight, weakness in bone, heart and blood circulation relation problems are the negative effect of the Sun.

Such people do not listen to anyone's advice and consider themselves supreme. They are not ready to change their ideas and plans under any circumstances and expect others to accept them.

Chapter 4

Puranic Story related to the Sun

The stories written in our ancient texts is a simple story for the general public. They can read it for some enjoyment, but it has great hidden meaning for those who are looking for deep knowledge in their lives. Then these stories reveal many secrets. One such story about Sun and his wife Sanjana.

Sanjana was the daughter of the divine architect Vishwakarma, she was fascinated by the divine influence of the Sun. Therefore, Vishwakarma married his daughter to Sun. From this marriage Manu, Yama and Yami were born. Later in the story, it was told that due to not being able to bear the brightness of the Sun, Sanjana left the

Sun and went to do penance and in his place, she placed her replica shadow (Chaya) in the Sun's palace.

The story progresses and one day Sun realizes the truth and searches for his wife. After countless searches he met his wife who had taken the form of a mare. But Sun recognizes his wife, both reunited and return back to the palace.

The story indicates happening of the following events;

1. Sun's own wife Sanjana left him

2. Sun not able to recognize the entry of Chaya in his life

3. After many years both reunited

Astrological Meaning of the Story

Sun's zodiac sign is Leo and planet Venus represents the wife and Venus in Leo indicates separation from wife. The story says that due to splendor and heat of Sun, Sanjana feels uncomfortable living with him. Leo is considered a fiery sign and Venus is associated with love, beauty delicacy, and refinement. Venus in Leo indicates that such a person is unable to maintain a good relationship with his wife. Circumstances in their lives force them to separate and the wife of the person has to live a life of isolation and loneliness as Sanjana continues to live as a mare in the mountains and doing penance. There is a possibility that some other woman comes into that person's life unexpectedly and unknowingly as a shadow (Chaya) comes into Sun's life and takes Sanjana's place and Sun doesn't know when Sanjana has gone and when Chaya has entered in his life.

Just as the story says that after many years the Sun comes to know the truth, similarly after many years such a man again starts worrying about his wife and searches for her. No matter what condition his wife is in, he recognizes her and brings her with him. Venus being in Leo does not indicate a happy married life.

One should not take these mythological stories literally. Every story tells about human life in great depth and reveals many mysteries. This also indicates that we are not living in isolation on Earth. Everything here is connected and these planets and constellations have a great impact in our lives.

Chapter 5

Own, Exaltation and Debilitation Sign

5.1 Leo – The Own Sign of The Sun

The entire zodiac is divided into 12 signs among them Leo is the 5th sign and the sign of the Sun. As different elements exist on earth like a place of fresh water, ocean water, fiery places, muddy ground, fertile land, etc. In the same manner the sky has also divided into different elements like fire, earth, air and water and these elements decides the ownership, exaltation and debilitation of the planets.

Apart from this, the degree of the zodiac signs is also divided in male and female sex area. Leo is the only sign where the entire 30 degrees belongs to the male area.

There is no other sign which has full male element. Therefore, a fiery and a 100 percent male element fits perfectly for the ownership of the Sun and the king of the universe feels comfortable in this sign. Therefore, according to the author, the ancient sages have given the lordship of only one zodiac sign to the Sun.

5.2 Aries – The Exaltation Sign of The Sun

Sun gets exalted in Aries at 10 degrees. Now, the question arises why this degree is the exaltation degree of the Sun.

To understand this, we need to understand something about the nakshatras. The entire zodiac is divided into 27 parts, thus span of each nakshatra is 13 degrees 20 minutes. The first nakshatra is Ashwini which span is 13 degrees 20 minutes and Sun is exalted in this nakshatras at 10 degrees. The duration of 13 degrees 20 minutes is divided into 4 parts and each part is called pada which spans 3 degrees 20 minutes. After the first 13 degrees 20 minutes the next nakshatra Bharani starts which span is 13 degrees 20 minutes to 24 degrees 40 minutes in the sign of Aries.

At that degree where the planet feels extremely comfortable gets exalted and that degree where the planets feel highly uncomfortable and want to leave the place immediately gets debilitated.

We need to understand Bharani to understand the exaltation of the Sun.

The symbol of Bharani is Vagina (Yoni). It is a female sexual organ and it is the source of existence. It is a way of birth that is attached to the uterus and only a fertilized egg can enter it. The vagina is a place that allows entry of only one sperm out of millions of sperms.

In other words, we can say that Bharani is a castle whose walls does not allow to enter any outside object and the structure of gates is in such a manner that allow entry of only one and after that, it is closed. There is only one king in a kingdom and the symbol of Bharani shows that only one can enter it.

In the sky where the celestial yoni exits and millions of stars takes its birth, when the Sun reaches in front of the gate of the castle, it means one pada before the Bharani begins (10° in Ashwini) Sun identifies that on the next step there is a big castle where he can stay without any disturbances.

A king requires a strong and comfortable castle for his stay and Bharani is that castle which provides such place to the King Sun. Bharani is a castle and the king needs a castle for his stay. Hence, according to the author's opinion, the Sun becomes exalted at the entrance of the castle which is at 10° in Aries. In India, Sun enters Bharani nakshatra from 28th April to 12th May every year. This is the time when Sun is extremely powerful and the temperature is at its peak in the country.

5.3 Libra – The Sign of Debilitation

The king of the universe gets debilitated in Libra at 10°. The sign libra starts from 180° and Chitra nakshatra 3rd and 4th pada falls in libra. After that Swati nakshatra starts from 6° 40' to 20° 00' and the span of first pada of Swati is 6° 40' to 10° 00'. In this pada, Sun feels highly uncomfortable and gets debilitated. So, we need to understand the span of Swati and after that Vishakha nakshatra starts and Saturn which is enemy to the Sun gets exalted in the first pada of Vishakha nakshatra.

The energy of Swati works for balance, this energy works for perfection, and force the person to keep on repeating the same thing till the perfection comes. Swati is for honing the skills while the tendency of the Sun is forward movement, because Sun can't stay at one place. Sun cannot agree to do the same thing over and over again, so it does not support any activity that forces repetition, even if it is for honing skills. Every day is a new day, every moment is a new moment, nothing is repeated here, a new life begins with the Sun. Sun means a new creation and never going back.

Swati is for balance, when there is any gap emerge the deity of Swati, Vayu (Wind), immediately force the surrounding atmosphere to fill the gap. The Supreme Creator doesn't like such a place where he has to do a job of filling the gap. He is more interested in the activities of creation and He creates always new things with no repetition. That's why a baby takes its shape in the womb of a mother, where the walls of such a creation are strong enough that does not allow infiltration of any outside object.

When the Sun reaches at beginning of Swati nakshatra, he knows that the celestial atmosphere does not support his work. The sign of Libra is shown by a man with a scale. It is a place where market activity is strong, people take interest in buying and selling of goods. They are interested in negotiating prices where every ounce count. The movement of the scale is very important and buyers and sellers argue with each other to come to a point of agreement. When they see that one of the parties involved in the deal is dishonest, they start fighting, people fight for some money and get ready to kill and die.

This place is not for the Sun who is the greatest giver and 'The Supreme Creator'. He knows that he has reached a wrong place and he has to pass such a time. He has to wait to cross such a place and then regain his strength. He knows that he is the king but this place will not give me any respect. He who is a symbol of time also has to wait for his time to become strong. Hence, Sun in Libra makes the person very humble.

Chapter 6

The 12 Adityas

The 12 zodiac signs are ruled by 12 solar deities known as Adityas. The energy of these 12 Adityas are different from each other. Hence, the knowledge of such Aditya reveals many secrets as the soul is influenced by such Aditya in the month it has taken birth. This controlling energy of the Sun controls our inner resources as Sun is the symbol of our soul.

The Twelve Sun Gods

The twelve Adityas are different forms of the Lord Sun. It is the manifestation of the same energy in 12 different forms at different times. In the middle of every month, when the Sun changes its zodiac sign, the energy of the Sun changes and a different Aditya starts shining in the sky. The path shown by the Adityas is the path that every person should follow, it is the path that leads to happiness.

The 12 Adityas, their zodiac signs and months

No.	The 12 Adityas	Signs	Sun Transit Month	Lunar Month
1	Dhata	Aries	14-Apr to 15-May	Chaitra
2	Aryama	Taurus	15-May to 15-Jun	Vaishakh
3	Mitra	Gemini	15-Jun to 17-Jul	Jeth
4	Varuna	Cancer	17-Jul to 17-Aug	Ashadha
5	Indra	Leo	17-Aug to 17-Sep	Shravan
6	Vivasvan	Virgo	17-Sep to 18-Oct	Bhadrapada
7	Pushan	Libra	18-Oct to 17-Nov	Ashvini
8	Parjanya	Scorpio	17-Nov to 16-Dec	Kartak
9	Anshuman	Sagittarius	16-Dec to 14-Jan	Makshar
10	Bhaga	Capricorn	14-Jan to 13-Feb	Paush
11	Tvasta	Aquarius	13-Feb to 15-Mar	Magh
12	Vishnu	Pisces	15-Mar to 14-Apr	Phagan

Chapter 7

Important Characteristics of the Sun

The Sun is the source of light and energy on Earth. It moves in only one direction, never retrogrades, stay one month in a sign, and completes the entire zodiac in a year. It symbolizes the soul and represents positivity, confidence, courage, and vitality. It represents ego, self-esteem, power, and leadership. It represents the king or ruler, the government, high officials and the father.

A strong Sun gives strength to fight against all obstacles in life, but it also gives aggression. Such a person has a dominant attitude, he is straightforward and outspoken, but due to his self-centered tendencies, he thinks that he always takes the right decisions. Such a person wants to be the center of all actions.

A weak and afflicted Sun can cause lack of confidence, poor self-expression and inability to face challenges in life. Such a person easily gives up in front of problems and becomes unable to do anything alone in life. Such a person is of shy nature and tries to avoid the eyes of others.

7.1 Sun Symbolizes Number 1

The counting of the zodiac starts from Aries where Sun is exalted. There is only one Sun in the sky. So, every counting starts from one and it shows that everything begins from the Sun. Sun is the karaka of only one house and that is first house in the horoscope, it has only one sign and that is Leo.

One indicates alone, it is not loneliness but the person enjoys his own being. As Sun never afraid to wander alone in the sky, a person having strong Sun is his horoscope never afraid to go alone anywhere. Duality starts from two; hence, a person having weak Sun is always looking for support, he is always afraid to go alone.

In ancient Hindu temples we see that there is only a small door for entry in front of the God. Many times, this question arises in my mind that those who built big temples, how can they not build a big door? Later, I came to know the meaning behind it. Every person has to go alone before God, a small door of the temple indicates that the person has to go alone before God. When a person is not afraid of being alone then his Sun is strong and it is represented by number 1.

7.2 Sun Represents Creativity

Sun is the lord of the fifth house which is the house of creation; it is the house of children and our children is our creation. It is the house of romance; romance means the person like to spend his time there and feel pleasure in doing such an activity. It is not limited to affection with a person but it has a broader meaning, like a person can do romance with his hobbies and like to spend hours in doing a specific activity. Important creations are born out of intense romance. Greatest creation comes into existence when a person takes interest towards romancing with higher aspects of life.

Time disappears in romance and lovers have experienced this. The Sun represents time and the fifth house represents romance. Therefore, ancient texts say that time disappears in divine romance. When the seeker experiences the state of "ecstasy" then time vanishes forever for him.

7.3 Sun Represents Health and Medicine

Sun is the significator of health and medicine. It is the giver and sustainer of life. The rays of the rising sun are considered very important for health. It has unique healing properties for cardiovascular problems, anemia, jaundice and several other diseases. Sunlight is a mixture of seven colors emanating from the Sun and each color wave has its own healing properties. Therefore, the ancient texts prescribe worship of rising Sun.

7.4 Sun Indicates Blood

Sun along with Mars also indicates blood. Human blood is divided into four elements;

    i)   White blood cells are indicated by the Sun

    ii) Red blood cells are indicated by Mars

    iii) Plasma is indicated by the Moon, and

    iv) Total cells are indicated by Saturn

7.5 Sun is known as Cruel Planet

Astrology has divided the entire zodiac in 12 signs and the Sun takes 12 months to complete one cycle of zodiac and stays one month in one sign. During the transit, as the element of the sign changes the energy of the Sun also changes, it means the kind of energy depends on Nakshatra and sign the Sun is transiting. The energy of the Sun which is unbearable in summer and people try to avoid going out, changes in winter and people like to sit in sunlight.

Due to this quality of the Sun, ancient texts have written that Sun is a 'Krura graha' (Cruel Planet), but it is not considered as malefic planet. The quality of krura we can understand with the animal symbol of Leo and that is lion. Lion is a cruel animal but it is the tendency of this animal, lion does not show any mercy to other animal while he is on hunting because it is the question of his survival. But it never creates worthless wrong deeds like fox and jackal for his own benefit. The main job of lion is to protect the pride from any danger and other animals hesitate to go near to lion. The presence of lion creates fear to other animals and this fear creates separation, but lion is not opportunists like tiger.

Sun is known as cruel planet because it creates separation and the planets located in Leo also create separation. Leo which is a highly masculine sign is a dry sign and feminine qualities like bonds of love and affection are completely absent here. Therefore, planets in Leo indicate that distance is inevitable in the life of the native related to the matter of that planet. The energy of the Sun which piercing in the month of summer become pleasant in winter. In the same way, the king's wrath never lasts long. It is necessary when declaring war, but the king must remain calm when signing peaceful documents.

7.6 Sun Provides Immunity

Sun is the main source of power and immunity. The exposure to sunlight is essential to ensuring proper levels of circulating Vitamin D and boosts the immunity of the body, but more is harmful. Exposure to ultraviolet radiation (UVR) in sunlight has both beneficial and harmful effects on human health.

Sun is known as a cruel planet. It is beneficial at the beginning but later the same would become harmful. In the same way, one should not go very near to the King (Sun) and should not spend much time with him.

7.7 Sun Represents Pingala Nadi

The human spine is especially influenced by the Sun. Yoga speaks about three basic energy streams in the human body; i.e. i) Ida Nadi also known as Chandra Nadi represents the Moon, ii) Pingla Nadi also known as Surya

Nadi represents the Sun and iii) Sushumna Nadi also known as Saturn Nadi represents the Saturn.

7.8 Sun is the Greatest Giver

Sun is the greatest giver of the universe. A king can never demand anything from others. It is the quality of the king to give to his citizens. When a person selflessly gives something to others, he strengthens his Sun and adopts the quality of being a generous person. The greatest creator of the universe never refuses to give. The thinking of a person influenced by the high qualities of the Sun is never narrow. This is why charity is glorified.

7.9 Sun Forgives Others

Sun is the king and the king should have the power to forgive others. Pride and honor are most important for a king. A person with strong influence of Sun forgives even his enemies.

7.10 Morning Prayer to The Sun

To strengthen Sun and move towards on the path of light morning prayer to the Sun is important. When the sun comes in the morning, both the hands of the seeker are folded and the head bows. It is the surrender of the ego and every surrender takes the seeker closer to the light.

Therefore, morning prayer to the Sun is important. The seeker takes water in his hand and offers it to the Sun. Critics say that water cannot reach the Sun because it is millions of miles away and this operation is useless. In fact, they do not understand the meaning of why our ancient sages have been doing this for ages.

According to the author, this method teaches us to give. When both our hands offer water to the Sun in the morning, it is a giving posture due to which our mind becomes pure and calm like water. That man's race to snatch and rob from others in the world begins to end. One who starts the morning by giving and immersing his ego does not join the race of snatching. The qualities of a great giver start developing in him.

This bowed head and giving posture of hands has strong power to change a person completely. The gradually disappearing ego makes a person as pure as water. Therefore, giving water to the Sun is not to reach it but to melt our ego, and the one whose ego melts finds God, this is true prayer.

Sun is associated with the spiritual growth of a person. Therefore, for spiritual development we should worship Lord Sun daily and chant Gayatri Mantra.

Chapter 8

Sun in Different Signs

The position of the Sun in different zodiac signs reflects deeply about the character of a person. Sun is the soul and the position of the Sun in the birth chart of the person indicates that the soul has decided to stay in the zodiac sign which is the most pleasant zodiac sign for it out of all the twelve signs. The Moon sign represents the mind of a person and the mind controls the body.

Hence, the characteristics of the Moon sign are clearly visible in the personality of the person. The Sun symbol indicates the inherent desire of the soul. Therefore, the action taken by the person not only influenced by the mind, but the desire of the soul also matters.

The solar chart provides soul level characteristics. Every action done by a person affects his soul. Every act of contraction shrinks our soul and every act of expansion expands our soul. Human life is meant for expansion only. Swami Vivekananda has said, "Expansion is life, contraction is death." Those on the path of expansion must strictly reject any path of contraction and our presence on the path of expansion must not hurt others. Any work that causes pain to others is not the path to expansion. Such a person harms his soul and the biggest expansion is the expansion of the soul. Hence, if a person's Sun is affected then he cannot be a courageous person.

The twelve signs of the zodiac are divided into four elements and the position of the Sun in these elements tells about the journey of the soul so far and its inherent tendencies.

8.1 Sun in Elements

8.1.1 In Fire Signs

The three fire signs are: Aries, Leo and Sagittarius

Sun is a fiery planet that feels extremely comfortable in fire signs. Fire always moves upward, so Sun in a fire sign indicates an ambitious and courageous person who never thinks backwards. The fire sign represents inspiration, passion, warmth, idealism and impatience.

All three fire signs are masculine sign and a masculine planet in a masculine sign creates high energy with aggression. Fire indicates action, initiation and appetite. Fire creates isolation and the dominance of the fire sign displays the above-mentioned qualities of fire in a person and such a person does not like to mix with other people.

Fire is used for creation but it also burns, so it needs to be handled with utmost care. Fire needs fuel and it has power to change things. It indicates drive for achievement and a desire to bring about radical changes. Therefore, these people take interest in creative activities and when the fuel is high their energy is also high.

Fire attracts attention as well as creates fear. Sun in fire signs indicates that these people attract attention with their presence and work but always maintain distance from others. They are willing to help others, but they are not social and friendly people. At present, we can understand the behavior of such people that they are not very active on social media platforms and they rarely comment. Sun in fire signs creates aloofness and also from social media platforms.

The fire sign is suitable for aggressive jobs and where initiation is important, but not for jobs related to negotiation, sales and marketing.

8.1.2 In Earth Signs

The three earth signs are: Taurus, Virgo and Capricorn

Earth means solid base, when something is related to earth then it is grounded and structured. It shows a person with a stable mind who always believe in practical approach and prefer facts and figures before taking decision. Such people avoid taking unnecessary risks and prefer to secure things first. Earth provides prosperity but hard work is required for produce. Therefore, the earth sign indicates a very hard-working person who moves forward step by step and is never in a hurry. They know how to utilize the available resources to achieve maximum output.

Sun represents movement and Earth represents stability. Sun in earth signs indicates that the person uses his energy for creative purposes. It indicates a very responsible and dedicated person who carries out responsibilities without any failure.

Earth energy is a feminine and receptive energy while Sun is a masculine planet. Sun being in the earth sign means that the person's aggression is reduced and he is of a polite nature. It also indicates slow pace with quality of patience. Earth belongs to material things; so, they want to enjoy luxurious life and work hard to achieve it.

Earth sign is suitable for responsible jobs; they are strong supporters and can give good suggestions but are unable to take initiation.

8.1.3 In Air Signs

The three air signs are: Gemini, Libra and Aquarius

Air is a dynamic element; it indicates an active personality who is involved in many intellectual activities. Air does not stay at one place, it indicates liberation and freedom. If air stops at one place, it starts rotting, and the flowing air always gives a feeling of freshness. The position of the Sun in air signs shows that they are intellectual people and prefer innovative ideas in life. They get bored easily with monotonous things; they like change and are always looking for something new and exciting in life. It is very difficult for these kinds of people to do the same kind of work at same place during their whole life.

If the total weightage of air element is high in the horoscope then such people do not stick to one principle, they change things rapidly and every change makes them feel like fresh air in life. It also indicates a fickle minded person who lacks the quality of patience and wants to see the result of his efforts in a short period of time. When there is a delay in getting the results of their work, they get nervous and leave the work midway. They own the latest gadgets that can get things done easier and faster and look for shortcuts in life. They want to stay updated with every information so they use high quality gadgets and are good at networking.

They give priority to movement and like the air spreads and changes its place very quickly, they quickly make their identity with their work but it is difficult for them to stay in one place for a long time.

Air signs are good for intellectual work, but they are not responsible people and lack stability. Air indicates desire, if the desire for completion of work is over then they immediately leave it.

8.1.4 In Water Signs

The three water signs are; Cancer, Scorpio and Pisces

Water is essential for life, its basic quality is to clean things and make pious. Sun in water signs indicates nurturing quality of the person. Water is very sensitive; hence, they are sensitive people and have strong gut-feeling. They are very emotional person and quickly catch the change in feelings. It is difficult to hide the feelings and intentions from these people, they immediately sense a person's hidden objective. They like to help others and take interest in charitable activities.

They believe in building strong bonds but they are mysterious people, do not open up easily and hide their thoughts and feelings. Safety is always important for them, because water needs a vessel. They check the safety first and foremost.

When it comes to buying something like a house or a car, they always give priority to maximum safety features, therefore, they always prefer to buy top model car. They check the safety and comfort of a place or chair before sitting on it. They like to keep themselves safe and avoid taking unnecessary risks.

Water indicates depth in personality, they are keen observers and nothing escapes from their notice. Due to the fluid quality of water it also indicates a very moody person. Water has the quality of freshness; they take care of every member of the family and prefer light jokes in their discussions to make the atmosphere pleasant.

Water signs are good for nurturing; their memory is sharp and remembers events after many years but they are not aggressive person and always hesitate to take initiation.

While analyzing the horoscope, proper balance of all four elements (fire, earth, air, and water) is necessary, only then it indicates a person with a balanced mind.

8.2 Sun in Signs

8.2.1 Sun in Aries

Aries is the first sign of the zodiac and the Sun is exalted in this sign. It is a movable and Kshatriya (warrior) sign ruled by Mars. The position of the Sun here shows that such a person has leadership and initiation qualities. They attract attention with their work but extreme heat is dangerous, so they can also cause harm. Very nearness to the heat is not good, it can burn you at any time.

The highest power of the Sun indicates high level of confidence. They are action-oriented person, willing to take risk and want to be at the forefront of everything.

The quality of this sign is dharma (righteousness). It is the duty of the king to protect dharma; Therefore, Sun in this sign indicates protection of dharma at any cost, such a person is ready to sacrifice anything for the fulfillment of his duty and think that whatever he is doing is for a very noble cause. These people are motivators, who give inspirational speeches in a passionate style which attracts the attention of others.

A warrior caste sign represents the spirit of fighting. When the energy is high the level of fight is also high. Sun indicates a strong fighting spirit and the person is ready to fight till its last breath.

Their action is very fast and intense. They are impulsive and want to see results of their efforts quickly. They are egoistic person and always feel confident in their decisions. Such persons do not listen to the advice of others and think that they always take the right decisions. Sun in Aries bestows many qualities on a person, when the energy is high then a stable mind and pious personality is required otherwise it can create great disaster. Adolf Hitler's Sun was in Aries and the influence of the fire sign was very strong in his horoscope and everyone knows his story.

Nakshatras included in this zodiac are Ashwini, Bharani, and Krittika 1st pada. Sun in Ashwini represents a work-oriented person who believes in the fulfillment of duty and runs hard for it. They are very energetic person and do not like to sit at one place for a long time. Sun in Bharani indicates a very creative person who removes impurities and sometimes even becomes furious to remove it. Sun is very powerful in this Nakshatra and these people are capable of carrying out big responsibilities. Sun in Krittika (1st pada) is very sharp and penetrating. These people use their power to protect others. They become very aggressive if someone challenges them.

Affliction: They are arrogant people, make every small thing a question of their reputation and quarrel fiercely. They are explosive and can get angry over anything. They behave like dictators and think they always make the right decisions.

8.2.2 Sun in Taurus

Taurus is the first earthy sign ruled by Venus. It is feminine, fixed and vaishya (merchant) caste sign. Artha (economic values) are always important for Taureans, so the energy of the Sun in this sign is work for material level. Being the sign of Venus love, beauty and art are always important. Sun's energy works for creative purposes and the focus of these purposes is on feminine qualities. The presence of women reduces the aggression of men, they stop abusing and fighting with each other in the presence of women and prefer to do those things by which they can attract women's attention. This feminine quality is visible in the person and this is the meaning of Sun coming into Taurus.

Taurus is a very sensual, sensitive and emotional zodiac sign. Therefore, Moon, the planet of love and affection, becomes exalted here. Nakshatras included in this sign are Krittika 2nd, 3rd and 4th pada, Rohini and Mrigashira 1st and 2nd pada. Krittika indicates that this energy serves for protection. Sun in Krittika (Taurus part) indicates that the keys of power have passed into the hands of the Queen and Sun in Krittika (Aries part) indicates that the keys of power have passed into the hands of the King. Hence, the difference between masculine and feminine energy is clearly visible when Sun is placed in Krittika (Aries part) and Krittika (Taurus part).

We can understand the position of the Sun in Rohini as the entry of the king into a very beautiful garden where people are singing and dancing, joking and laughing. A pleasant and cool breeze is blowing and everyone looks very happy. The atmosphere forces even the king to participate and dance in it and in this situation the king cannot take any tough decision.

Mrigashira indicates search and the Sun's energy in this position works to discover better things in life. These people do not compromise with anything less than the standard quality and are willing to spend more to get the finest things. They are willing to travel far to eat at a fancy restaurant and prefer going to a party where expensive food and drinks are served.

Affliction: The pursuit of sensual pleasures and focus on luxury may become their sole purpose in life. They become highly conservative and reserved individuals who stay in their own circle and do not like to change anything in life. They become lazy and greedy persons who always think about money and sensual pleasures.

8.2.3 Sun in Gemini

Gemini is a dual and sattvic sign whose lord is Mercury. This is an odd, masculine and barren sign. The duality of Gemini indicates two energies operating in the same space. Like both male and female are living under the same roof. When two people live under one roof, both have to accept all the positivity and negativity of each other, only then harmony is possible. It indicates acceptance, adjustment, respect and providing space for the other's existence.

Sun in Gemini indicates a person who is ready to adjust for everything. They analyze quickly the possible space in negotiations and turn the conversation toward agreement. They find the midway and work to bring peace. Hence, they are good is sales and marketing because they are able to convince people with their intelligence. It indicates a person who has good command on language and communication. They are quick, spontaneous people and like to visit places. They prefer variety in life and believe that only change is constant. They are good in making connections and Sun in Gemini indicates that such a person makes good relation with seniors and authorities.

Nakshatras included in this zodiac sign are Mrigashira 3rd and 4th phase, Ardra and Punarvasu 1st, 2nd and 3rd phase. Sun in Mrigashira indicates a person whose focus is on quest. It indicates the pursuit of knowledge and they are willing to travel anywhere to increase it.

Ardra is wet and Sun in Ardra is indicative of an emotional person. They do not care about others and do whatever they want to do in life. Sun in Punarvasu means endless energy to try again; they never get disappointed in life and use their intelligence to overcome the circumstances.

Affliction: They are very indecisive persons and lack the quality of concentration. They are only interested in gossip and show unnecessary curiosity in the affairs of others. They use their intelligence to deceive people and fulfilling their desires becomes their top priority.

8.2.4 Sun in Cancer

It is a rajasic and mutable sign whose lord is the Moon. It is a watery and feminine sign in which the Sun cannot be aggressive, hence, it indicates a very kind and gentle person. Male planets in female signs are not able to show their aggression because men try to look civilized in the presence of women.

Apart from being creative, they are also emotional people. They follow their heart and believe in nurturing others. The fresh water of Cancer sign indicates a loyal and loving personality who has strong bonds with his family and is committed to his friends. They always keep their surroundings fresh and clean and take special care of the thing they like the most.

Sun in this sign indicates a person who seeks comfort in every aspect of life. They like to listen to melodious music while sitting on a luxury chair. They are sensitive people and feel easily hurt by lack of attention or loud noises from others. They are sophisticated people and do everything with utmost care. Water dissolves everything; hence they are mysterious people, easily digest emotions and secrets and always laugh in front of others. It is very difficult to know what is inside their mind because there is depth in the water.

Nakshatras included in this zodiac sign are Punarvasu 4th Pada, Pushya and Ashlesha. Sun in Punarvasu indicates a person who is not aggressive and uses gentle words, such a person is always ready to cooperate with others. Sun in Pushya indicates a selfless, gentle and philanthropic person. He believes in everyone's development and works for the upliftment of others. Sun in Ashlesha indicates a person who is protective by nature, like a snake coils for its protection, they create a circle and do everything for protection. This means securing a home, securing children, securing a job. Creating a circle means that no outsider is allowed, it also means that there is no leakage of information related to security measures.

Affliction: They are very moody persons and are always indecisive. They like to postpone tasks that involve decisions and like to follow others but cannot move forward alone. They feel lonely, quickly become frustrated and unable to cope with difficult circumstances. They become overprotective and check the safety of the same thing multiple times.

8.2.5 Sun in Leo

Leo is the fifth and own zodiac sign of the Sun. This is a fixed sign that shows that such a person sticks to his words. Once he says something, he always sticks to it. It is tamasic and Kshatriya caste sign. Sun is Leo indicates a great desire for creation. It indicates a strong and determined person with strong fundamental qualities. They want to live life with full enjoyment.

Leo represents mountains or caves and present day we can understand it a separated cabin or room where another person does not easily approach or think twice before approaching. The symbol of Leo is Lion; hence, Sun in Leo indicates a lion is sitting in his mountain caves. It indicates that such a person doesn't like any interference in their work and others can see his presence only when he comes out from their caves (room). These people get deeply involved in the process of creation (in their work) and they do it will full passion.

A positive and fiery sign indicates, they are very confident and outspoken person. It indicates honor, pride and loyalty and utmost level. Leo is all about expression, they want to show their creation and talent to the world. Hence, they are aggressive, and like to take initiative.

Nakshatras included in this sign are Magha, Purva Phalguni and Uttara Phalguni first pada. When Sun placed in Magha then such a person respects his roots and ancestors. Sun in Purva Phalguni indicates a fun-loving person who is full with passion and takes interest in singing and dancing. Uttara Phalguni indicates a very hard-working person who never frustrates under any circumstances.

Affliction: These are very selfish and egoistic people. They avoid doing any negative acts themselves, but involve the other person in doing it for them. They are autocratic people and don't like to hear the word "No". They use force to fulfill their desires and become fierce.

8.2.6 Sun in Virgo

The second earthy sign is a dual sign ruled by Mercury. This virgin sign represents feminine aspects of 'Nature'. Virginity represents cleanliness and purity. Placement of Sun in this sign represents the enhancement of feminine qualities. These people focus is on purity and until the things become completely clean and pure they repeat the process. It also indicates a perfectionist who works hard for better output.

In this sign the energy of the Sun works to produce new and innovative ideas and Mercury indicates business and communication. Virgo is an even and sattvic sign. It is barren and vaishya (merchant) caste sign. The placement of Sun in an even and sattvic sign indicates pious behavior with patience to achieve their objective. A barren and merchant sign indicates that on the matter of business and money they become greedy and rude and their focus is always on how to maximize profits.

Nakshatras included in this sign are Uttara Phalguni 2nd, 3rd, and 4th pada, Hasta and Chitra 1st, and 2nd pada. Sun in Uttara Phalguni indicates a courageous and hard-working person. They are very dedicated person and find their own way to achieve their goal. Hasta means hand, Sun in Hasta means such a person has some skill in their hands. They have strong finance and marketing skills and quickly analyze the movement of money. Their behavior is always cordial and they always look for possible business opportunities.

When Sun is placed in Chitra (Virgo part) its focus is on intelligence rather than appearance. We can understand it with the making of jewellery. The first part is its manufacturing where intelligence is required to prepare a beautiful piece and the second part is after the creation now it has gone to the showroom where people can see and admire its beauty but no one knows the artist who created it.

Affliction: They are very stubborn and don't like to change their opinion. They use their intelligence for wrong purposes. They take undue advantage of their relations and deceit people because many people like his cordial behavior. They are scammers, hackers, and online fraudsters etc., because their focus is always how to gain money by wrongful means and become quick rich.

8.2.7 Sun in Libra

The Libra symbol, the scales, represents harmony and fairness. Sun in Libra indicates that this energy works to bring balance and justice. They work to bring equilibrium; hence, they are interested in proper solutions rather than useless debates and fights. Libra is an airy, rajasic, and masculine sign ruled by Saturn the enemy of the Sun.

Here the power of Sun is reduced, so they are not aggressive people rather they use diplomacy to resolve the matter. Libra is the 7th sign in the zodiac and this is where the search for a partner begins. Air indicates intelligence, rajas indicate passion and masculine character indicates initiation. In this sign, Sun represents an intelligent person who works hard to achieve his goal. They are very social people and have good relations with everyone.

Nakshatras included in this sign are Chitra 3rd and 4th pada, Swati and Vishakha 1st, 2nd, and 3rd pada. Chitra (Libra part) indicates that they are extrovert person and their focus is on flamboyant objectives. They want to show their talent to the world and never work behind the curtains. Sun in Chitra (3rd and 4th pada) means that the market is important, so such a person focuses on pomp and show, he takes interest in showing off his goods.

Sun in Swati indicates a flexible and soft-spoken person who quickly adapts to changing surroundings. They love to travel and business is their top priority. Sun in Vishakha indicates a competitive personality who works very hard to achieve their goal. These people compete tough with their rivals, they have a strong desire to be at the number one position and to reach there they use all kinds of methods, whether right or wrong.

Affliction: They are unable to maintain balance which leads to disharmony, upset, worried, stressed and disturbed nature. They are always looking for a partner and make many partners and because of the air sign they never stick with anyone. They keep moving around and changing their partners. They are unable to take decisions, hence; often they delay the matter as they are not sure about the consequences or avoid facing it.

8.2.8 Sun in Scorpio

Scorpio is an auspicious and feminine sign ruled by Mars. It is a fixed, watery and Brahmin caste sign. It is a tamasic sign and represents a hiding place. When water is fixed at a place then it starts doing down and after some time it becomes muddy. This sign does not support the quality of flow of water; hence, placement of Sun in this sign indicates a stubborn person. They have inherent quality of hiding and probing. They are quick to analyze the hidden motives of the person. They are tough and fit themselves in any situation in life. They are secretive and mysterious person who keep many things below the surface.

They do such things for years that even the person closest to them is not aware of. They like to work on secret projects and work hard to gather secret knowledge. They take interest in occult and learn many secret things. They like to discuss secret and taboo topics, work on them and gather a lot of information.

Nakshatras included in this sign are Vishakha 4th pada, Anuradha, and Jyeshtha. Sun in Vishakha shows that these people do not let others win easily, give tough competition, struggle for years and want to win at any cost. They are careful in every step they take and wait patiently for the right time. Sun in Anuradha indicates that the person faces many challenges in life but they never get discouraged and are always ready to fight the circumstances. They never give up and emerge victorious after many struggles. Sun in Jyeshtha indicates that they work to secure things before any unexpected event. They do everything perfectly and never rush anything.

Affliction: They become obsessed with achieving their goals and do not hesitate to adopt unfair means in life. They are cunning, vindictive and cruel person. They are jealous and possessive person. They look for their own benefit in every situation and when circumstances are not in their favour, they change their commitments.

8.2.9 Sun in Sagittarius

King Sun is now in the sign of Jupiter who is the advisor of the gods. It is the duty of the king to follow the advice of Jupiter who always shows the right direction. The presence of Sun in this sign indicates an intelligent person with philosophical inclinations. They have a strong ability to think deeply and provide strong suggestions. Sun in Sagittarius shows that the person likes challenges in his life and every challenge enhances his personality. It indicates a pious person with a high level of religious inclination.

The fire of Sagittarius represents the thirst for knowledge; they are sattvic by nature and dharma (duty) is always important for them. Sagittarius indicates treasury or military position and the position of Sun in this zodiac sign indicates that such a person does a treasury related job or work as a military advisor. These people have a strong ability to guide people and provide the right direction.

Therefore, they provide direction for investment, finance or military related training. They take keen interest in all kinds of works where hitting the target is always important, as the Sagittarius sign is related to the bow. The strong ability of this placement is to quickly analyze the situation and find an optimal solution. Sun in this sign indicates very religious and highly educated people who undertake long journeys.

Sagittarius sign includes Moola, Purva Ashadha and Uttara Ashadha first pada. Sun in Moola indicates a very straightforward person with a sharp mind. They have good knowledge of medicines and are capable of solving complex cases. Sun in Purva Ashadha indicates a strong fighting spirit that does not accept defeat under any circumstances. They remain optimistic even in extremely negative circumstances. Such a person has a strong ability to change the game and win the battle with minimum resources. Sun in Uttara Ashadha indicates a very committed person who never leaves anything in between and completes the task at any cost.

Affliction: They may deviate from the path of righteousness and become obsessed with achieving their goals. They become vengeful person and this high energy is only for their revenge rather than focusing on the search for truth.

Sun in all three fire signs indicates high energy of a person who has a controlling attitude towards others and does not like rebels. Therefore, they do not hear anything against themselves and take strict action if they are in power. It also indicates the low level of receptivity of a person who always considers himself supreme.

Fire has the power to create but it can also burn. When energy is high, extreme caution is required. Dealing with high energy requires a high level of responsibility otherwise it can go in the wrong direction at any time.

Following are the differences between the three fire signs;

Aries: Movable, Rajasic, and Kshatriya caste sign. Action is always important for them and they prefer to take initiative.

Leo: Fixed, Tamasic, and Kshatriya caste sign. Self-confidence and desire to create are important and they become determined.

Sagittarius: Dual, Sattvic and Kshatriya caste sign. A Mutable sign indicates transformation from animal to human. Knowledge is important and they are ready to do anything for wisdom.

8.2.10 Sun in Capricorn

It is the third earthy sign and ruled by Saturn. It is a movable and feminine sign. The quality of this sign is artha (economic values) and the caste is vaishya (merchant). Sun in Capricorn indicates a very realistic person who doesn't want anything superficial and ambiguous in their surroundings.

They are good planners and do everything in an organized and constructive manner. They are able to undertake great responsibilities and fulfill it diligently.

Capricorn is the strongest earthy sign and these people know how to utilize every available resource to get the maximum result. Sun in Capricorn indicates strong power to control and put restrictions. Such a person focus is on rules and regulations and they follow it with strictness. They are good to preserve things and save every ounce to achieve their task. It indicates a solid person who achieves their aim amid various difficulties. Saturn a slow-moving planet represents obstacles, hence, movement in their life is slow and they achieve their goal but after crossing many hindrances.

Nakshatras included in this sign are Uttara Ashadha 2nd, 3rd, and 4th pada; Sharavana and Dhanishta 1st and 2nd pada. Sun in Uttara Ashadha indicates an adventurous person who fights fiercely from the circumstance until they win. Sun in Shravana Nakshatra indicates focus is on sound and that requires quality of attention. These people don't like worthless chattering and pay full attention to their work. Sun in Dhanishta indicates focus is on restrictions and creating harmony. They like musical instruments and prefer to beat drum.

Affliction: They become stick to their belief and thoughts and probability of following the obsolete and irrelevant rules for years. They don't like change and always stick with their thoughts and become furious when someone opposes it.

Following are the differences between the three earthy signs;

Taurus: Fixed, Tamasic and Vaishya caste sign. A fixed sign indicates stubbornness and a hard-working person to the material gains.

Virgo: Dual, Sattvic and Vaishya caste sign. A dual sign indicates for material gains person will do negotiations. Such people say some price and finalize the deal on some other price.

Capricorn: Movable, Rajasic and Vaishya caste sign. These people observe the matter carefully, make proper plans, never rush and act only when the time is opportune.

8.2.11 Sun in Aquarius

The third air sign of the zodiac is a tamasic and fixed sign ruled by Saturn. This air sign represents innovation and progress and the position of the Sun indicates a magnanimous person who likes to work on humanitarian aspects and adopt a philanthropic approach. They are creative, determined and unconventional person.

They are futuristic individuals who generate out-of-the-box ideas and being an air sign, they do not like limitations. They take interest in technologies and create revolutionary gadgets and mobile applications and bring new change. Their focus is always on change and they try various new and innovative ways to achieve their objective.

The tamasic and fixed sign indicates a silent worker who has the ability to work at one place for a long time, it also indicates no movement of the person. These people have strong capacity to control their senses and become mystics and a hermit who sit at one place in meditation for long hours.

Nakshatras included in this zodiac sign are Dhanishta third and fourth pada, Shatabhisha and Purva Bhadrapada first, second and third pada. Sun in Dhanishta indicates that the person's focus is on restrictions to bring harmony in a disturbed situation.

Sun in Shatabhisha indicates that such a person adopts hundreds of methods to get the answer. They take bold decisions in life and return only when they have the answer.

Sun in Purva Bhadrapada means that such a person does not hesitate to destroy old and obsolete things and throws away all the dead things immediately. This indicates a highly alert person who immediately recognizes any malpractice and stops forwarding dead things even if there is a mistake in the document. This indicates a deep investigation of the documents. For example, having a wrong date in a document spoils the document and perhaps no one else can catch it, but a person whose Sun is in Purva Bhadrapada catches it immediately.

Affliction: They become very moody, eccentric, and rebellious person and always take interest in unconventional ideas. They are unable to bring harmony and impose too many limitations and restrictions which further worsen the situation. Instead of controlling their senses they want to control others and instead of sitting for meditation they sit to create destructive things. They are not willing to listen to anyone and only create destruction in the name of revolution, with the feeling that all their actions are noble.

Following are the differences between the three airy signs;

Gemini: Dual, Sattvic and Shudra caste sign. Here the focus is on cooperation, peace and maximum effort to satisfy the individual. No one can complain about the efforts made by these people for satisfaction.

Libra: Movable, Rajasic, and Shudra caste sign. The focus here is on movement, action and to increase output for maximum gain. To increase business, they have capacity to travel a lot.

Aquarius: Fixed, Tamasic, and Shudra caste sign. Sitting for long periods of time, working alone and waiting for the right time to complete the work indicates patience for results.

8.2.12 Sun in Pisces

Pisces is a dual and sattvic sign ruled by Jupiter. This third watery sign indicates compassion and sensitivity. Sun in Pisces indicates a humble person; they like to help others and try to avoid tough competition. They are philosophical and are interested in religion and spirituality. They take interest in many creative activities. It indicates imagination and fantasy and they take interest in all the works related to it, hence they work in the field of media and entertainment. They like to work on fantasy novels, plays, films and in the present time they create animation with the help of computers which looks at par with reality. They live in a world of imagination and create various imaginary characters that seem real.

Nakshatras included in this sign are Purva Bhadrapada 4th pada, Uttara Bhadrapada, and Revati. Sun in Purva Bhadrapada shows that this energy works for creative destruction. They believe in radical change and adopt new methods to achieve their objective. This energy gives birth to either a highly spiritual person or a ruthless person who silently uses his mind only for destructive purposes.

Sun in Uttara Bhadrapada indicates a very hardworking person who believes in taking rational decisions. Their writing quality is excellent but they hesitate to speak at first because they are not aggressive people. Sun in Revati indicates a person who likes to travel for successful meeting. They are very social person, love jokes and work as a comedian.

Affliction: They adopt every wrong method to achieve their objective and consume alcohol and drugs heavily. They are very lazy people, always away from the real world. They live in a dream world, unable to distinguish between illusion and reality.

Following are the differences between the three watery signs;

Cancer: Movable, Rajasic and Brahmin caste sign. It indicates a person who is polite and non-aggressive. Brahmin caste indicates that they think deeply before taking any step. They are open people, have a clean heart and like cleanliness in their surroundings.

Scorpio: Fixed, Tamasic and Brahmin caste sign. It indicates a person who works secretly and in the dark. They think deeply but never reveal their thoughts and plans to others. They are always secretive people.

Pisces: Dual, Sattvic and Brahmin caste sign. It is a changeable sign; hence, it is adaptable but there is a possibility of both growth and decline. On the higher aspect it indicates a pure sattvic person, but on the lower aspect it indicates a ruthless person who looks very nice, talks religious things and commits crimes.

Chapter 9

Sun in Different Houses

There are various aspects of human life and the twelve houses of astrology represent every aspect. These twelve houses include everything that can happen in a person's life. We are part of this vast expanse and there is nothing separate here. Everything is connected and the invisible energy of nine planets have complete control over us.

Sun is a source of continuous energy. Strong Sun shows that such a person never despairs and deals effectively with adversities in his life. The position of the Sun in the horoscope plays an important role in a person's life. It is the source of light and indicates that it is present in all areas associated with that house (bhava). Therefore, things related to that house have a deep impact on the personality of a person and it also indicates the inherent character of that person.

Sun provides us warmth and protects us from cold. Presence of Sun means absence of cold and dullness, therefore, matters related to that house where Sun is located are always active and cannot remain cold. Each soul chooses its own body that represents its form, the scriptures say that the soul is the form of God. Every soul is unique hence every person is unique and the position of the Sun has a deep impact on the soul as well as our body.

The planets move anti-clockwise in the horoscope and at 6 in the morning the Sun in the ascendant and remains in one house for two hours. At 12 noon it is on the 10th house which is the zenith point, at 6 pm it is on the 7th house and at 12 midnight it is on the 4th house, which is the nadir point of the zodiac.

The time of birth reflects the position of the Sun in that house. Therefore, it is said that each soul chooses the time of its birth, it is the house where the soul finds most comfortable to live in this life, because no one wants to live in a house that they do not like. In other words, the soul itself has selected that house of the Sun on the basis of the karma of the previous life. Nature keeps track of everything and whatever we get from nature including body and mind depends on all our actions.

9.1 Sun in the First House

The first house represents our body stature. Sun gets directional strength in the first house. Sun in the first house indicates a controlled energy and such a person is very strong in bearing pain. Due to heat in the head, they have less hair and get angry easily. They are stubborn and prefer to remain isolated from others. They work with the government or hold some official position in life and live a respectable life.

'First' signifies novelty and originality. Such a person has strong will power and is determined to achieve his objective. Sun gives life, it represents optimism, positivity and a strong will to live. Such a person wants to live life to the fullest and remove all kinds of negativity. They are enthusiastic people and give powerful speeches. It points to a leader who energizes his colleagues with his forceful speeches.

They are quite energetic and passionate person and do not hesitate to take initiative. They are very enthusiastic people and carve their own path in life. They speed up the completion of work, show leadership qualities and people follow their orders.

They are courageous people and have a strong will to overcome obstacles. When work is present they are extremely active otherwise they remain in their separate rooms just like a lion lives in his cave and does not want any disturbance in his rest.

Affliction: They are power-seeking people and have autocratic tendencies. They always want to take credit for everything they do and often say, "I did this and I did that..." and the "I" is always important in every sentence. They are extremely arrogant people, far from humility, who have false pride and always consider themselves supreme. Their focus is on personal achievements rather than generosity and they become highly self-centered individuals.

9.2 Sun in the Second House

It is the house of traditions, wealth and savings. Sun in the second house indicates a broad-minded person who is attached to his family and likes to follow his traditions. The emphasis of such a person always remains on financial security. The desire to accumulate material wealth is very strong in their life and for this they work very hard.

Savings means accumulation of wealth. In present days we can consider it with accumulation of stocks and shares, bonds, property and other exchangeable assets that can be converted into wealth. They know how to utilize the available resources and have strong sense of business, they quickly recognize opportunities that translate into earnings as their focus is always on increasing wealth. Savings always becomes their top priority and their focus is always on how to maximize it.

The second, sixth and tenth houses are known as earth (wealth) triangle houses, and the placement of Sun indicates a good and stable career in life. They are highly career oriented individuals as it relates to one's wealth and social status. They are talented person, work very hard and hone new skills so that they can earn more. Their focus is always on accumulation of material things.

They are generous people and help others with money. They are economical and willing to travel miles to save a few bucks, they look for various options of discount and are ready to wait for a huge seasonal discount to buy a product. Savings is always important for them because Sun is placed in the house of savings. They are ready to spend money on good food as it is also the house of food and grains. Their memory is strong and Sun in this house bestows the quality of oratory and singing but other combinations are also important.

Affliction: To save more they become extremely frugal and do not like to spend even a single penny for others, but for themselves they eat expensive food and spend on luxurious items. They believe only in wealth accumulation and material success in life. They show their items to others which makes them feel successful in life. They may have vision and speech-related problems.

9.3 Sun in the Third House

It is the house of adventure, communication and travel. They are good at documentation and writing and present their ideas well in written form. They are well versed in all modern types of communication; Mobile phones, email, television and social media platforms, etc. They never like to do a desk job all day long, rather they want to meet new people, express their thoughts in emphatic words and build a healthy relationship with others. They have many friends and know how to build a good network with people. This is the house of siblings and their relations with them are always good, but sometimes their uncompromising nature can become a cause of trouble.

They are very active people and are ready to travel at any time. They are ready to go anywhere for their work, take short trips throughout the day and feel energetic during the journey. But when documents and travel are absent they feel lethargic and prefer to relax only. In fact, communication, documents and travel are the three lifelines for these people.

They are courageous people and do not hesitate to step forward on unknown paths, but they are also not blind risk takers. It indicates a very mature person who exercises his power and takes steps only after analyzing all the pros and cons of the situation. They take up big responsibilities in life and never leave any work midway. They face every situation courageously and never compromise with their dignity.

Affliction: They keep wandering here and there without any proper guidance and keep themselves busy in useless activities. They take unnecessary risks without properly analyzing the situation and try to run away from their responsibilities. They are unable to manage their files, keep bundles of documents on their desks and do everything haphazardly.

9.4 Sun in the Fourth House

This is the house of our family, home and happiness. Sun in the fourth house shows that they are deeply attached to their family and take care of every person. They are very fond of their mother because the fourth house is the house of mother. They are always cautious about domestic matters and take care of everything in their house. They are introverts, prefer to stay at home and work from home.

Fourth house indicates heart which means love, it is associated with our strongest emotions; hence, they love their home and find happiness in doing the tasks where fourth lord is situated. Sun in the fourth house indicates a liberal and compassionate person. This is the house of early education and they take interest in reading and perform better in college education.

Sun is the king and the king cannot live in a small house. Therefore, they prefer to live in a bigger house and are ready to travel but they are not ready to accept living in a smaller house which may be closer to their workplace.

This is the nadir point (lowest point) of the zodiac and the Sun transits into this house at midnight. During this time the sunlight focuses not on the outside world but on deeper things. It indicates a person who searches for hidden things in life. They are interested in secret things and like to solve mysteries. They quickly understand human psychology because every hidden and mysterious thing fascinates them. This type of behavior makes them different from others because they like to spend their time in esoteric things, hence they have fewer friends. Sun at nadir point creates a strong foundation.

Success is difficult at an early age in the life for these people because the Sun is exactly opposite to the tenth house, which is the house of social status. Therefore, it takes time for them to create their social identity. They are not interested in showing their work to others and people are not ready to recognize their research work easily. They do not like to run after people for any recognition, hence they lag behind in social life. They are less active on social media and do not take interest in commenting. But as time passes, the Sun slowly begins to shine; hence, the second half of their lives is completely different from their first half.

This is the house of the grave, indicating the spiritual nature of the person who takes interest in matters related to death and likes to unravel the mysteries related to it. They are not materialistic, interested in gaining in-depth knowledge and are willing to sacrifice in pursuit of the unknown. The Sun at the nadir point means that their priority is to go to the lowest level to find the truth. They are more interested in knowing things deeply rather than showing off their achievements.

Affliction: Sun represents the ruling nature of the person and they want to control every matter and behave like a dictator in their home. Privacy is always important to them and they do not allow others to touch their things. Their mysterious behavior creates isolation and separation from other members of the family.

9.5 Sun in the Fifth House

The fifth house is of creation and the greatest creator is now in his own house. It shows high level of creativity of the person and these people are always engaged in some kind of work. They have artistic talent, like to perform on stage and take interest in cultural activities. They are generous and joyful people and feel great intimacy to their children.

They are adventurous people and are not afraid to take any new step in life. They work for the development of new things, where innovation is always their top priority. Since every day is always a new day, the focus is always on novelty and they don't like to copy and paste ideas.

This is the house of speculation, gambling, betting and broking. They perform better in calculating risks and take good decisions about investments. They are expressive individuals, interested in sports and want to show their talents to the world. Placement of the fifth lord indicates association of that house to the activities of creation.

Affliction: To earn more they make risky investments and believe in the high risk, high return principle. They become addicted to gambling and forget that Rahu can swallow the Sun completely, meaning they can lose their entire investment or bet.

If the fifth house is affected by a malefic planet then they do not want to work hard for creation and prefer to copy or steal the work of others. They do not have the courage to walk alone and always seek the company of others.

9.6 Sun in the Sixth House

It is the house of competition, conflict and struggle. Sun is an abundant source of power; it indicates a person who fights with all his courage to win. These people give tough challenges to their opponents and never compromise in a losing situation. They fight with full courage in every situation of life.

It is the house of immunity and diseases and Sun indicates strong immunity. They take interest in medicine and join medical profession because Sun is the greatest healer, its rays kill bacteria, cure diseases and make the person healthy. Hence, they are very health conscious people and keep a strict control on their diet.

Health means not only individual health but also the health of the society. They like to study subjects related to sociology, political science, law and medicine and take interest in matters related to politics, society or public. They like to bring issues that are affecting the society in front of the public and actively participate in all these matters.

They are very active on social media and TV shows and discusses personal health as well as how to improve society. For better health, they are in favor of removing all those things which hinder it, whether it is related to food habits, rules and regulations or social stereotypes. They actively participate in cultural programs and manage with enthusiasm. They do charity events, organize donation camps and visit villages to raise awareness. They write articles and create videos on matters that directly affect the public at large. They are courageous people and show leadership qualities.

Affliction: An afflicted Sun indicates that the person easily accepts defeat in life, does not have the ability to fight the situation, loses vitality and leads a depressed life. Their immunity is weak and they are unable to digest food. They are of quarrelsome nature and are always ready to fight. They bring every small matter to court and fight in vain but winning for every fight is always important for them.

9.7 Sun in the Seventh House

Sun shows its evening position in the seventh house. When the sun sets, its rays become pleasant and bearable. People feel relaxed after a busy day. Sun in the seventh house shows the joyful nature of the person. They like to help others and take interest in soft and melodious songs. They want a partner who can bring social prestige in their life. They are good at building relationships and want company over tea. They want complete acceptance from their partner and express displeasure when anything is refused. They perform better in a team than alone.

This is the house of marriage and partnerships and they are looking for loyal and helpful partners. Sun in this house indicates a gentle soul. They love to share their food and easily give up their morsel. They do not like any kind of rudeness; hence, they are unable to tolerate the rude and harsh behavior. Being of soft nature, they expect the same behavior from others, but the world is not the same. The rude behavior of others has a deep impact on their life as they stay away from any kind of harshness and aggression. Sun in the seventh house creates distance in relationships.

When a traveler returns in the evening after a journey started in the morning, he has a wonderful experience of the day. Sun in the seventh house indicates that such a person has to go through many experiences in life. This requires a mature soul and their life forces them to become a very mature person.

Affliction: An afflicted Sun indicates trouble in relationships. They get anxious easily, become weak in transactions and get fooled by others because they are not able to understand business contracts and agreements. They lack self-confidence and are always looking for support. They lack initiation of any kind and wait for others to get things done for them.

9.8 Sun in the Eighth House

It is a secret house and represents all the hidden things in our life. The Sun in this house indicates a person who takes an interest in solving things that are not easily visible on the surface. They take an interest in the dark and mysterious world and study occult subjects. They are explorers and enjoy finding hidden things.

Since they are interested in deep things they do not like to discuss their matters with anyone. Since they are not sociable people, they have very few friends. The "Mystery" is their true friend and they are busy searching for it. Therefore, anything mysterious always attracts them.

They work for those departments where things are kept confidential. It is the house of transformation; hence, they witness drastic changes in life. This house represents inheritance and wealth from legacies. It represents the wealth of the partner and the strong Sun indicates good support from in-laws.

The energy in this house moves towards knowing the truth behind the curtain. Therefore, they always take an interest in uncovering the dark and mysterious things of life. With their strong investigative power, they can identify the root cause of the problem. They can easily detect fraud and manipulation in documents. No matter how neatly a forged document is made, it cannot escape their notice. They catch the hidden intentions of the person and take an interest in exposing the forbidden things in life. They may experience betrayal in their life as it is the house of secret affairs.

Affliction: An afflicted Sun indicates underworld activities. They become very active at night and do their work only in darkness. They never forget to take revenge even after years. They become criminals who use such energy to harm others in a covert manner. They become addicted to sex, seek only negative things in life, and keep everything secret and below the ground.

9.9 Sun in the Ninth House

It is the house of fortune, religion, father, faith, and wisdom. Sun in this house indicates a noble and pious person who takes an interest in religious activities. These people are deeply connected to their father and guru and follow the path shown by them in life. The energy of this house works for religion and the pursuit of knowledge. Therefore, they are very intelligent people and have religious faith in life.

The ninth house indicates higher education and long journeys. They are highly educated people and undertake long journeys to study and gather various types of knowledge. They are scholars and dynamic speakers. They are true to their word and like to follow rules in life. They believe in foundation and make efforts to strengthen it.

It is the house of printing and publishing. Therefore, they take an interest in all these matters or work in a publishing company. They are experts in some fields and like to travel for discovery and exploration. They are social and helpful people and like to do charity. They work as heads of departments of educational institutions, professors, judges, or priests.

Affliction: An afflicted Sun indicates fundamentalists who believe in the supremacy of their religion and faith. They are conservative persons who do not want to change their rules throughout their lives. They do not listen to anyone's advice and their relations with their father or guru are bad. They use their knowledge and intelligence for wrong purposes with the belief that they are doing the right thing. They always look out for their own benefit and help others but only for their own benefit.

9.10 Sun in the Tenth House

This is the house of a person's career and social status. This is the highest point of the zodiac and the Sun transits this point every day at noon. There is abundant sunlight during this time, indicating that activities related to the tenth house cannot be hidden and their work immediately becomes visible to others.

Sun in the tenth house indicates that success in career comes easily in their life. The maturity age of Sun is 22 years; hence, they start their career around this age. They work very hard to brighten their career and turn every adverse situation in their favor. Time is always important to them; they are punctual and they work in businesses where perfection matters.

Sun indicates heat and excess heat creates separation. Strong Sun indicates an authoritative position where the person sits alone in his cabin the whole day and remains isolated from others. They are highly active individuals during the day who don't even have time for lunch. They work in key positions in the government department where their decisions affect many other people. They do not want to do research and investigative activities, rather they want to be in the limelight and show their talent to the world. As their actions come to light, one day their misdeeds also come to light. The Sun is here and nothing related to it can be hidden.

Affliction: An afflicted Sun indicates that they do not mind using unfair means in life to achieve success. It is important for them to be in the limelight, so they put their face forward in everything they do. They become egoistic and want credit for every work. The word "I" becomes very important to them and appears in abundance in their conversations. Ego creates heat and heat creates distance, so people start avoiding them. They do not want to leave their post at any cost and as soon as they leave their post, they fall seriously ill.

9.11 Sun in the Eleventh House

It is the house of income, profits, and aspirations. When Sun comes to the 11th house it is the morning time after 8 a.m. and Sun remains here for next two hours. It is the time when activity increased in the world. It is the time to plan for the day, do business and generate income. In India, at this time businessmen prefer deal in cash and do not like to lend. Therefore, there is more desire in the 11th house than in the 7th and 3rd house. Sun in this house indicates high aspirations with good source of income.

It is the house of hopes, desires, friendship and social activities. They work for things related to public welfare and charitable schemes. They are always optimistic people and spread hope in the lives of others. They like fun and often say jokes in their discussions. They have many friends and a strong professional network. They network with high status people and are quite active on social media. Social status is important to them and their network is their asset.

Since their focus is on income, they have more than one source of income. They build good relationships with everyone and respond quickly to questions. Therefore, they act as spokespersons or representatives of an organization. They are an active person on television and express their views on various topics. They are team players and perform better in groups but are unable to manage independently.

Affliction: This is the house of desires and they can do anything to fulfill their desires. Afflicted Sun indicates that they use their networks and communication channels to woo people and fulfill their desires. They spread wrong information in the media for their own benefit. They are always busy with their friends' and want any kind of engagement even that has no meaning.

9.12 Sun in the Twelfth House

The Sun rises in the ascendant and it is morning time. After this it goes to the 12th house and stays there for two hours. It is the house of loss, expenditure and salvation. This is the time when business activities are nil and people are getting ready to go to their work. This is the time to make yourself aware, this is the time to make yourself healthy, this is the time to worship Lord Sun and not think and discuss about business and income.

Therefore, it is the house of loss and salvation. This house represents monasteries, seclusion, confinement, hospitals and asylum.

Sun in this house indicates inclination towards spirituality. It is the house of hidden places, secrets and the subconscious mind. Sleep and dreams are related to our subconscious mind; hence it is the house of sleep and dreams. Sun here gives loss of sleep, so these natives work for night duty in hospitals and other places. They help people prepare for their work and engage in activities that make a person healthy. The king helps the one seeking asylum; hence, these people are of generous nature and always ready to help others.

The 12th house represents the secret workings of the human mind. It indicates hidden enemies, conspiracy, deceit, fraud and deception. The presence of Sun indicates that they quickly understand the hidden nature of a person.

This is the house of foreign travel and settling abroad, if other aspects of the horoscope support them then there is a possibility of going and settling abroad. They have a good understanding of art and culture and take interest in all those activities. Because this is the house of subconscious mind, they are good at imagination and are involved in those activities where strong imagination power is required.

Planets in 12th house put a person in isolation. Benefic planets indicate search for deeper meaning in life and malefic planets indicate solitude and confinement.

Affliction: Afflicted Sun indicates loss of respect in life. This is the house of imprisonment and the influence of inauspicious planets can isolate the person, it can be either a prison or a home or a hospital bed.

Chapter 10

Sun with Other Planets

Sun is the king and his conjunction with other planets is like a king sitting in his court with his various ministers. In the presence of the king, no minister is allowed to take independent decisions and only the king has the power to give orders. This does not mean that ministers have lost their presence and cannot do anything. The only thing is that they cannot give any order but they can give their valuable advice to the king and later the king can convert that advice into order. But in the presence of the king no minister can show his independent presence.

Before understanding the conjunction of other planets with the Sun, it is necessary to understand at what degree distance that planet is from the Sun and if it is close to the Sun then it is considered combust in astrology. It does not mean that all its power has been lost, rather it means that in the presence of the Sun it does not have the power to take decisions but it can advise the Sun. The combust planet shows that the Sun is not alone responsible for all the matters related to that house, but the advice of other planets also influences the decision taken by the Sun.

The planet which will be together at equal degrees near the Sun, that planet will be considered to be completely combust. The planet which is at a distance of 8 degrees from the Sun will be considered as half-combust and the planet which is at a distance of 15 degrees from the Sun will be considered as fully rising. (There are other opinions about these degrees but I consider the above degrees only.)

When the king is absent each minister has full power to take his own decisions. Similarly, when a planet is located at a distance of more than 15 degrees from the Sun, it independently influences the matters related to that house. There may be two or more planets deciding on matters related to that house, so their relationship with each other is very important.

If the relationship is friendly then both works together and the affairs of that house prosper, if they are neutral then they do not interfere in each other's work, if they are enemies then both try to dominate each other. It indicates chaotic situations in life and matters related to that house always trouble the native. There is a lack of harmony and peace in that house and no work is done smoothly. Such a person has to work very hard to make things fruitful and when he sees some stability, unrest comes again.

10.1 Sun - Moon

The Sun represents the masculine energy and the Moon represents the feminine energy of the universe. Both these energies are constantly working and cooperating with each other for the proper functioning of universal activities. The day is ruled by the Sun and at that time the masculine energy is powerful and the night is ruled by the Moon and at that time the feminine energy is powerful. The energy during the day supports action and aggression and the energy at night supports love and compassion.

Therefore, the Moon is powerful when it is away from the Sun, because when the Sun enters the Moon disappears. When the Moon is exactly opposite the Sun (at 180°) then it is a full moon day and the Moon is at full power, it can display its light to its full potential. The Moon is considered weak within 72 degrees of the Sun. Amavasya (New Moon) occurs when both the Sun and the Moon are in the same house and less than 13.2 degrees apart from each other.

Moon represents our mind and when there is no light in the moon it indicates lack of power of mind. It does not mean stupidity but it means that the mind is unable to face difficult situations in life. Such people get nervous easily, are always in dilemma and are unable to take decisive decisions. They say something, soon their mood changes and they say something else. Moon near the Sun indicates a person with an unstable mind. They are very emotional people, always looking for security around them and incapable of taking risks in life.

Due to the brightness of the Sun, the Moon becomes unable to show its presence in front of the Sun. In other words, she can't stand the heat of the Sun. The legend related to Sun and his wife states that his wife left him because she could not bear the heat of the Sun. Planets too close to the Sun lose their independence but the Moon disappears completely.

This combination indicates a polite person who stays away from mischievous activities. They are mild-mannered, happy-go-lucky people with no ulterior motives. However, they are easily influenced by the outside environment be it change in weather or conditions. Their immune system is weak and they fall ill easily. Moon also represents mother, so these people should always have a good relationship with their mother or motherly figure and should always serve them to strengthen their Moon.

10.2 Sun – Mars

We can understand the conjunction of Sun and Mars as if a king is standing with his generals. Both are masculine, aggressive and friendly planets. When a king stands with his generals, his power becomes immense, therefore, Sun is exalted in Aries which is sign of Mars. This energy makes a person confident, courageous and determined.

The king stands with his generals and discusses the state of the kingdom and gives orders for action. Therefore, the people with this type of conjunction have very active and aggressive personalities. This high energy does not let them sit still and they work hard to get the results of their work.

When energy of both the planets supports each other then it enhances the matter related to that house. It indicates a strong will and daring attitude of the person and they belong to army, police or other jobs where high energy is required.

They are ambitious person and desire to achieve power and authority in their life. They are impulsive, take decisions on the fly, and never shy away from taking initiative. Therefore, they are never afraid to face adverse situations in life. They are stubborn, do not listen to others' suggestions and always put their own decisions above all else.

When energy is in excess then it needs to be given proper direction; They perform better in athletics and other sports where correct channelization of high energy is required. Improper use of energy creates anger and destruction. They are ready for conflict at any time and fight fiercely. They take big risks and are never afraid of any opponent. This combination creates a combative personality and they want to win every challenge. They are not afraid to venture into unknown territory and they enjoy the thrill of the chase. They cannot sit still even when they do not have any clear direction in life. Due to excess energy they try in wrong direction and waste energy.

When energy is high it must always be in good hands otherwise disaster is possible. Therefore, to give proper direction to such energy a strong a well-placed Jupiter is required to show the way to the correct utilization of such energy.

10.3 Sun – Mercury

Sun is known as the father and Mercury is the prince who represents a young child. Wherever the child goes, his father is aware of his activities. In astrology Mercury cannot move more than 28 degrees away from the Sun and the Sun-Mercury conjunction is known as "Budhaditya Yoga".

Mercury is known as the messenger and significator of all types of communication. Many astrologers believe that Mercury never combust and I also believe in the same. A child's demands can influence a father's decision and the father cannot ignore them. In the same way, the decision of the Sun is influenced by the Mercury on the matters related to the house. This planet, which controls every type of communication, has full power to influence the decision taken by the Sun (soul).

Therefore, while analyzing this conjunction, it is necessary to analyze Mercury independently. Strong Mercury indicates a good grip in terms of communication while weak Mercury indicates problems. When Mercury is behind the Sun it indicates impulsive behavior and fast communication because when the child is behind the father he wants to come to the father quickly. When the father is behind the child, the child feels relaxed and plays with a calm mind and without any worries. When the Sun is behind Mercury the person deals with all matters related to communication calmly and avoids being hasty.

According to astrology, when the planets come near the Sun, their speed becomes very fast and when they move away from the Sun, their speed slows down. Therefore, Saturn, the most distant planet, teaches us patience because its speed is very slow.

Mercury represents the intelligence of a person. Strong Mercury indicates logical thinking and mathematical ability to the person. A child should grow up with his/her parents, without any proper guidance a child can easily get influenced by the mischievous people of the society. If Mercury is alone in the horoscope and is under influence of malefic planets, then such a person uses his intelligence only in negative activities.

10.4 Sun – Jupiter

Sun is the king and Jupiter is the Devguru and both are friends of each other, hence this conjunction produces fruitful results. These people are very optimistic and creative in nature with religious inclination. The decision taken by a king is always important as it affects the lives of many natives of his kingdom. Therefore, decisions for the benefit of the state should always be taken in collaboration with a very intelligent person and this combination indicates the same.

When the king and Jupiter come together then the king cannot take any hasty and inappropriate decisions because every decision is influenced by Jupiter and he represents wisdom. Jupiter indicates a person with wide knowledge who has experience in many directions and Sun is a royal planet. Both of these are collaborative forces and they work where the individual provides his guidance and opinion on important matters. Therefore, this combination creates a very intelligent person who directs the energy in the right direction for the proper functioning and well-being of the people.

These natives work as professors, priests, chief advisors to the government, etc. They provide their valuable suggestions to the government or the person in charge for taking decisions. This combination creates a natural counselor whose job is to distribute his knowledge to people and provide the right direction.

In case of afflictions, these people misguide others for their own benefit. They misjudge the situation and suggest wrong conclusions which make the situation worse. They become arrogant about their knowledge and always try to dominate others.

10.5 Sun – Venus

According to astrology, the relationship between Sun and Venus is inimical. Venus is said to be the lord of arts and represents feminine qualities. While King Sun is a masculine and krura (fierce) planet. Venus is the hottest planet due to the presence of carbon dioxide, clouds and acid, while Mercury is the planet closest to the Sun.

Despite being the hottest planet, Venus has gentle qualities and is considered the goddess of love. Love is very delicate, it has tenderness and cannot be treated strictly. Love is like a fresh flower and it withers as soon as it hardens. Just like we have to hold a fresh flower with delicate hands, love also requires the same delicacy. Sun is bold and forceful having no soft qualities and there is no place for tender feelings near it. Ruling a kingdom requires taking tough decisions and toughness is exactly the opposite of Venus's nature. Therefore, these are two different energies where the symmetry is completely missing. Hence, a person having this conjunction has to face tough situations in life.

Venus wants art, music and love and Sun is devoid of all these qualities. People with this conjunction tend to have the qualities of Venus but they have to face difficult situations in life where their soft qualities do not take shape because all these qualities are absent in the Sun. Hence, their efforts go in vain.

Sun is the hot planet which represents action and dryness and Venus is the soft planet which represents politeness and freshness. Venus is the ruler of fresh water, a very close combination indicates that water evaporates and dryness remains.

Therefore, Venus feels uncomfortable in displaying its qualities and becomes suppressed if it is combusted. When Venus passes over the Sun in transit it indicates that all the water on Venus has dried up. Water indicates not only emotions but also relationships and bonds. A close conjunction between Sun and Venus indicates relationship is dried.

This conjunction indicates that Venus's softness gradually begins to dry up in various circumstances of their lives. If the conjunction falls in the 7th house, the person with this combination has tender qualities but he may face tough behavior from his partner whose reactions may dry his tender tendencies. Whenever they want softness in life, they always get a harsh answer. Slowly, the flower of tenderness starts withering from their lives.

Venus wants to enjoy the joys and luxuries of life but Sun is always busy with matters of state (work) and does not have time for all these activities. It shows that the person wants to enjoy luxuries but circumstances do not support him. Gradually, the tender feelings of Venus begin to dry up. Venus always avoids quarrel and turmoil at any cost, and tries to lead a happy and peaceful life, but Sun shows arrogance and anger.

The qualities of these two planets are totally differed from each other. A person with this conjunction wants to live a peaceful life which he does not get. Sun is extremely fierce planet and Venus is extremely soft planet, due to the difference in the basic nature of both, the combination of both spoils the matter of that house. No matter how many differences exist between these two planets, Venus does not go beyond 48 degrees from the Sun.

Therefore, before doing any analysis it is necessary to check the distance between these two planets. If the distance between the Sun and Venus is more than 43 degrees and 20 minutes then it indicates delay in marriage.

A very close conjunction to Sun and Venus also causes eye problems. I have seen in my experience that a person gets glasses late in life whose difference between Sun and Venus is more than 28 degrees. If this difference is less than 5 degrees then vision weakens quickly. Venus represents transparent glasses then he has to take help of glasses. A person with weak Venus is unable to handle delicate glasses and often breaks them.

We can understand this combination from some more examples from life. In the presence of women, men like to show their gentle behavior to attract their attention. They stop fighting and abusing each other and wait for the woman to leave the place. The mere presence of a single woman has the power to change the heat of the discussion because no man wants to expose his absurd behavior to a woman. Similarly, the presence of Venus affects the decisions taken by the Sun. Sun cannot be rude in presence of Venus. Hence, this combination enhances the creative qualities of the person and makes the person soft, gentle and humble.

These people are interested in love, art, music, fashion and like to eat rich and tasty food. Venus is a very sophisticated planet which shows that gentle behavior, manners and etiquette are their top priority and this conjunction indicates a person with such qualities. But these people have to face dryness in love related matters because a close conjunction indicates that the water of Venus evaporates. However, a close conjunction to Sun is good for spirituality. When Venus is far from Sun it indicates more water that means an emotional person. Such a person is good at building relationships and maintains strong bonds with his friends and family. They are not ready to leave those people to whom they love.

Their negative side is that they are very emotional, even small things hurt them. They spend more than their capacity and show off unnecessarily.

10.6 Sun – Saturn

Sun is the soul which represents light and Saturn is the main ruler of death and represents darkness. These are two opposite energies. According to astrology, the relationship between Sun and Saturn is inimical. When planets with opposite energies meet in any house of the horoscope then they do not support each other and start dominating to show their supremacy and this creates disturbance in the matter of that house. For example, Sun is the indicator of time and Saturn is the indicator of the end of time.

Hence, this combination shows that the watch of such a person will never work properly, either he will lose it or it will get damaged. The poor watch has been gone in the fight between Sun and Saturn. There is another meaning of this conjunction. Damage of watch indicates damage of time, the Sun–Saturn conjunction indicates a delay in time. Therefore, there is a delay in things happening and nothing happens on time in their lives.

Following are some more differences for better understanding of these two energies;

1. Sun is a fiery planet, due to its influence things become hot, active and agile. Saturn is a cold planet, due to its influence things become freeze and isolated, speed slows down and every activity stops.

2. Sun is the king and Saturn is the guard. When the king arrives, the doors are opened and the guard's job is to close and lock the doors. When the Sun comes in the morning the darkness goes away,

when the Sun goes in the evening the darkness returns. These two are opposite functions and both cannot happen simultaneously.

3. Sun is the beginning of activity and Saturn brings limits, restrictions and takes things to their end; Saturn is "The End".

4. Sun represents autocracy and Saturn represents democracy.

5. Sun shows ego and Saturn brings down every ego. Saturn shows the real truth of life and makes the person humble by removing all types of ego.

Hence, this combination indicates overcoming ego because Saturn means being devoid of ego. Saturn creates many obstacles to reduce the ego, this shows that the more ego a person has, the more obstacles he will have to face in his life. Saturn is an emotionless planet which teaches discipline and hard work in life. This combination makes the person extremely practical who stays away from all kinds of gossip and manipulation.

Rahu work as an agent to Saturn and has full power to engulf the Sun i.e., remove light in the life of the person. Therefore, giving up ego and becoming a humble person is the only key to overcome the negative effects of this conjunction. If this conjunction occurs in Aries then it indicates a high ego whereas if it occurs in Libra then it indicates a humble person.

Sun represents father and authority and Saturn who is his son represents masses and working-class people. Saturn is the planet of justice and brings balance. The judge shows no mercy while giving justice. That is why Saturn shows no mercy to the Sun and destroys all its negativity. This combination indicates that the person will not have a cordial relationship with his bosses and will challenge his superiors for any wrong doing.

It indicates wild arguments between father or authority figure and in transit the situation become worst. Therefore, the career of these individuals is inconsistent as both Sun and Saturn are the karakas of the tenth house which is the house of career and the fight between these two, spoils the career like a watch gone haywire in the above example.

In the house in which this conjunction occurs, the person has to face various obstacles. For example, if this conjunction falls in the fifth house then the person faces problems in his creativity and the child is our creation. Hence, such a person has to face problems in marital life or children related problems.

If this combination comes in the fourth or tenth house in the horoscope of a native, then it is not good for his professional life. He has to face a lot of struggle to make his way. The aspect of these two planets with each other in the fourth and tenth houses also creates a lot of struggle in the native's professional life and he gets initial success in his career after a lot of struggle. The maturity age of Sun is 22 years and the maturity age of Saturn is 36 years. Hence, the life of such a person between the age of 22 to 36 years is full of struggle.

The Positive Thing

The positive thing is that this combination gives birth to a very mature person. However, many kinds of obstacles come in their life but they are always ready to fight them. They tend to be self-made individuals and achieve success through their own efforts, although their learning curve may be longer than others. They become down to earth people and are ready to remove darkness from life. They remain isolated from others, become spiritual and take interest in occult. On the higher aspect, this combination indicates that the person will seek the light but will have to go on the path of darkness and one cannot move towards the light without seeing the real truth of life where the biggest obstacle is one's ego.

On the Downside

The downside is that they become undisciplined and pessimistic individuals who lack goals in life. Instead of becoming humble, they become timid, avoid challenges and do not have the courage to face adversities.

10.6.1 Difference Between Saturn and Pluto

We need to differentiate between the functioning of Saturn and Pluto, both of which are considered karaka (significator) of death, so what is the difference between these two deaths. I am writing my experience below;

There are two types of death, first is the person's own death and the karaka of that death is Saturn and second is the death that the person can see with his eyes and the karaka of that death is Pluto. Therefore, Saturn has an impact on the person himself, but Pluto's impact is much broader than that. Whatever death we see with our eyes is caused by Pluto but for ourselves it is caused by Saturn.

10.7 Sun – Rahu

Both Sun and Rahu are enemies of each other. Sun is the king of light and Rahu is the king of illusion and darkness. When light comes, darkness automatically goes away. There are two types of darkness, the first is that in which a person knows that he is in darkness. One who is aware about his darkness seeks light, Saturn represents that darkness. As such, the seeker of truth knows that he is in darkness and he keeps wandering here and there in search of light. The second is that darkness which a person does not even realize that he is in darkness. He believes only in snatching and looting things from others like, fraudsters, hackers, thieves, robbers etc. They have no realization that they are living in darkness, that darkness is ruled by Rahu.

When Sun rises in the morning, the darkness of the night automatically disappears. In fact, it disappears even before the Sun comes over the horizon. So, Rahu cannot be present where Sun is present but the voice of the soul (Sun) can be suppressed by material desires (Rahu) and giving priority to material desires is to strengthen Rahu.

Rahu is a disturbed energy, in which house it presents it creates disturbances. The close association of a planet with Rahu indicates that planet always get disturbed and that bring many ups and downs in life. One should never try for shortcuts to get success in life, because it disappears soon, anything given by Rahu disappears quickly, Rahu is never reliable.

On the day of the eclipse, Rahu has the full power to swallow the Sun, which shows that one can push back one's soul to satisfy one's material desires. But the soul is immortal and Rahu cannot defeat it. Therefore, during an eclipse, the Sun disappears from the sky only for a short period of time. Following are some more differences between these two energies;

1. Sun represents sattva while Rahu is a master of sin.

2. Sun is the giver while Rahu has no intention to give anything, it is always taker.

3. Sun is the king and makes rules while Rahu is rebellious and enjoy to break the rules.

4. Sun follow the righteous path while Rahu always take interest in mischievous paths and shortcuts to achieve the desire.

5. Sun is forthright while Rahu is conspiratorial.

The combination of Sun and Rahu in astrology in known as grahan dosh. When the two opposite energies meet at one place, the life of the person is not a smooth life. It gives birth to many difficulties and the person has to face a lot of struggle in his life. It indicates difficulty to father and when Rahu transit in the sign of Leo or over the Sun such difficulties arises after the age of 42 years.

To overcome the negatives of this conjunction, one should never pursue one's material desires and should always give priority to religious activities. Rahu movement is opposite to that of other planets i.e., he does not like to follow traditional paths, thinks in the opposite language and likes to go against the order. But Rahu needs the help of others to act because he does not have hands and legs, hence, he influences other planets with his thoughts.

Sun - Rahu conjunction means that the energy of the Sun is influenced by Rahu. Hence, the thinking and actions of such a person are different from others. This combination shows that the person will not support old and conservative ideas and will bring changes in the system. He will put forth new and revolutionary ideas which may not be accepted by the traditional followers but he can never support conventions of the society. Therefore, this combination gives birth to rebels and revolutionaries.

The downside is that malicious desire of a person can swallow the piousness of the person and he is force by his desire to follow the path of darkness. They become power hungry people and misuse their authority to fulfill his desire. They always adopt rebellious attitude towards government or father and enjoy creating trouble for others.

10.8 Sun – Ketu

Ketu – The South Node of the Moon, known as the planet of separation which means end of all attachment. When one thing is separated from another it destroys all types of communication and relationships. The person is not interested in meeting people, going for parties; hence, Ketu represents silence. Ketu is a fiery planet and the place where it has influence starts drying up and becomes barren. It is a mysterious planet and gives birth to unexpected events in life.

Rahu means running after desire and Ketu means that the person has the experience of running after desire. Ketu indicates that the person does not take any interest in the matters related to that house as he has no attachment to it.

For example, when Ketu is placed in the tenth house the person has no attachment to his workplace. He is doing his work because he has to, but when the time is up he does not like to sit in the office even for a minute more. While Rahu in the tenth house shows a desirous and workaholic person who sit for long hours.

Ketu indicates victory, but every victory requires hard work and sacrifices. Ketu has no attachment, it indicates that the person does not hesitate to sacrifice those things to achieve success where Ketu is placed. For example, Ketu in the 4th house indicates that the person stays most of the time out of his home and do sacrifices related with the 4th house to achieve purpose of his life.

Ketu has no head, it represents hidden things and the ability to penetrate. Ketu is not interested in show-off activities, it provides energy to the person to go deeper and find hidden truths. That is why these people are very good at researching and finding secrets and the biggest mystery is the "Creator" of the universe himself. The scriptures say that it is present everywhere but we cannot see it with these physical eyes.

This shows that there is some power in the body of every human being whose development makes the person enlightened and as that capacity increases, the person becomes capable of knowing the invisible and in common parlance it is called intuition. Therefore, Ketu is the planet of intuition, spirituality and enlightenment. Enlightenment cannot be seen with these physical eyes; therefore, Ketu has no aspects.

This combination shows that the person takes interest in spirituality and stays away from unnecessary wandering in worldly affairs. Ketu cuts off every negative influence of the Sun present inside the person and makes the person a seeker of truth. Ketu brings many changes in life and forces the person to follow the path which is his true purpose. Therefore, Ketu can influence the Sun partially, but not completely, hence, the Sun-Ketu conjunction forms a partial solar eclipse.

These people find success in fields that require the ability to uncover hidden secrets. They are proficient in astrology, palmistry and other secret sciences and dive into the ocean of spirituality after the age of 49.

Sun and Ketu both are fiery planets and Ketu indicates explosion. It indicates excessive heat in the house where this conjunction occurs and if it occurs in a fiery sign the situation can be dire. If the person does not channel such energy into spirituality then it can cause great harm.

The negative side is that they lack patience, are indecisive and get restless easily. They lack self-confidence, go into depression and isolate themselves from others. Instead of finding positive activities they take interest in negative activities and while doing so they are able to hide their real face from others because Ketu has no face.

Chapter 11

Transit of the Sun

Transit means when one object passes in front of another object in space. The planets are revolving around the Sun which is revolving around some other unknown celestial body along with its entire solar system. There are two different theories that attempt to explain the organization and movement of celestial bodies in the universe.

The first is geocentric and the second is heliocentric. The geocentric model states that the Earth is at the center of the universe, and the planets, Sun, and stars revolve around it. Heliocentric models consider the Sun as the center and the planets revolve around the Sun. Since, we are using the term transit of the Sun, therefore, we go for the geocentric model and assume that the Sun is moving.

Sun is the main source of every activity in the world. Due to its immense heat and light nothing can remain motionless, weak and stagnant. Sunlight brings the seeds sleeping in the ground out of their dormant state. A small plant collects energy from the Sun and grows into a huge tree. Similarly, every year on the day of birth when the Sun transits over the natal Sun the person gathers energy and feels energetic and alive. This is why we feel happy when our birth date approaches. Our soul receives energy from the Sun and expands. Therefore, worshiping Lord Sun not only provides energy but also happiness, because energy brings happiness.

Absence of sunlight means absence of energy, and less energy brings sadness or despair in life. Therefore, when a person goes into depression, he starts avoiding sunlight. He likes to keep himself in the dark where sunlight does not come. When a seed does not get sunlight, its growth stops, similarly when a person avoids sunlight, negativity automatically starts coming in his mind.

Sun means activity, when Sun transits over the natal planet, due to the heat of the Sun, every planet gets energy and becomes active and also activates that house where it is placed. Therefore, the transit of Sun on natal planets plays a very important role in a person's life. For example, if Mars is placed in the fourth house and the time when the Sun will transits over natal Mars then the activities related to the fourth house will increase. The end result may be positive or negative, depending on the relationship between the transiting Sun, the natal planet and the house element.

Sun means awakening and going to work and Moon means returning home and rest. Therefore, people go to work in the morning when the Sun rises and return from work in the evening when the Moon rises. When the Sun enters the zodiac sign, the constellations associated with it become active and we get to see its results. The energy of the constellation which is active affects the Earth. I have explained the Sun's ingress into each nakshatra in my book "The Light of Nakshatras".

11.1 Transit of Other Planets on the Natal Sun

When a slow-moving planet passes over the natal Sun, the activities of the house in which the Sun is present are affected. However, the outcome of these activities depends on the relationship of that transiting planet with the Sun. For example, if the natal Sun is in the fourth house and Jupiter is transiting over it, then such a person takes interest in reading religious texts at home and others activities related with wisdom. If Saturn is transiting on the natal Sun then the matter of the fourth house becomes active and such a person may see change of the house or place during that period.

11.2 Eclipse

Eclipse is an important astronomical event and in astrology it is an important event that brings many changes and it deeply affects humans, society and country. It is important to consider in which Nakshatra the eclipse is taking place and if any natal planet is present in that Nakshatra, then a conjunction of less than five degrees is considered inauspicious.

Eclipses occur every year and the maximum number of solar and lunar eclipses in a year is seven. The question arises why eclipse is considered inauspicious?

The Sun represents the masculine energy of the universe and the Moon represents the feminine energy of the universe. It is only through the union of these two energies the process of creation continues in the world.

Both of them are auspicious energies which protect the world from inauspiciousness. In the universe, not only good spirits are present but evil spirits are also present and they are looking for a chance to be born on earth, because nature prevents very lowly spirits from taking birth. During an eclipse, auspicious energy is absent from the environment for some time and these evil spirits get a chance to fulfill their desires.

Therefore, negative events, diseases, accidents and deaths increase around the eclipse. Hence, doing any auspicious work at the time of eclipse is prohibited and giving birth to life is an extremely auspicious work which takes the human life forward. Therefore, sex is prohibited at the time of eclipse because auspicious energy is absent at that time and inauspicious energy can give birth to a crippled, impotent, criminal, murderer and an extremely cruel person.

Chapter 12

Nakshatra of the Sun

In Vedic astrology, the lordship of Krittika, Uttara Phalguni and Uttara Ashadha has been given to the Sun. Sun is the source of energy and represents life force. The dominance of these three Nakshatras over the Sun shows that the energy level in these Nakshatras is very high. High energy is required to complete any difficult task. When the resources are less and the goal is big then a lot of energy is required, because if the energy is less, then the person gets disappointed soon but if it is the never-ending energy of the Sun then the person never gets disappointed and moves ahead with self-confidence. Therefore, these three nakshatras represent high energy and abundant self-confidence.

These people are able to handle difficult situations in life and where others think victory is impossible, they emerge victorious. Their life gives them challenges because difficult tasks are given only to those who have the courage to complete them. In fact, every difficult task provides an opportunity to gather energy and achieve the goal. Sun is the hero of the universe and the nakshatras of Sun provide a heroic personality to the person and the deeds done by these heroes are remembered by the people for centuries.

I have written in detail about all 27 Nakshatras in my book "The Light of Nakshatras". Following are some excerpts from the book about the Nakshatras of Sun;

12.1 Krittika

Krittika is the 3rd of 27 nakshatras and situated at 26°402 Aries – 10° Taurus. It is a cluster of six stars depicted as nymphs acting as nurses of "Lord Kartikeya - The god of war". The word Krittika is divided into "Kriti" and "Ka". Kriti means "Creation", "Work done", "Action" or "Creative work has done by someone" and "Ka" is a preposition of relation. Therefore, the word Krittika means relation among the cluster of six stars and that relation is only for creation and for a specific aim or object. When the six stars focus on only one goal, their energy is very sharp and penetrating. Hence, another meaning of Krittika is "The Cutter".

Symbol: The symbol of the constellation is a sharp object as a kind of razor or knife or axe or anything which has a sharp edge. The tip of the flame is sharp since hot air rises. The symbol represents the intense nature of the Nakshatra; its energy is very sharp and has strong ability to penetrate deeply.

The symbol indicates that Krittika people never hesitate to cut anything but being protective in nature they never take the initiative to harm others. When they find something wrong or there is no point in keeping it, they are ready to cut it without any hesitation. Just as a sharp arrow can pierce the target, they always do only purposeful and meaningful things. If the arrow has no target, they never shoot it from their bow i.e., they do not indulge in doing anything worthlessly. They don't like to wander here and there and always do something which has a purpose in life. They don't like gossip and say only a few words, they believe in saying short sentences and don't like lengthy discussions and meetings. Their discussion aims to get straight to the point, and they don't like to circumrotate.

Caste: The caste assigned to the constellation is 'Brahmin'. A Brahmin is a person who works on his mind and can think deeply. They are knowledgeable and visionary person, and have a strong ability to guide others. The caste indicates an inclination towards purification. Although it is a very aggressive nakshatra, they never fight for anything wrong and believe that what they are doing is always right.

Characteristics: Krittika's energy is a very high fiery energy. When the energy is high it can't sit idle. These people never hesitate to take initiative; they are adventurous and never afraid to take step towards the unknown path. Due to their penetrating insight and ability to play with sharp objects, they properly assess the depth of the risk and prepare their planning accordingly.

As the symbol of knife indicates, their logics are very sharp and with their penetrating eyes they can see the hidden truth or hidden motive of a person. Their focus is always on a direction and immediately cut all those things which have lost its direction. In a meeting they cut the worthless discussions, they cut the relations; they leave their work and place without hesitation. They are the first who speak in a meeting and when no one dare to ask, they ask questions and as the fire is visible from a long distance, they get attracted immediately. This energy is a unique mix of sharpness and softness, they are very aggressive people but their personality also has softness and they never use their aggression for wrong deeds. The fiery energy of Krittika never does any harm to anyone unless it is teased. This energy always works for protection.

They can catch a flying knife by their hands but they keep its sharp edge always down and raise only when danger arises. They are very sharp but on face always appear to be a soft and polite person. They like calm and peace in their surroundings.

Krittika's natives are not afraid of trials; being courageous they always take their step forward and want to see the outcome from their eyes. They lack consistency and want to enrich their experience, so, they leave their job, they leave their city and country too. Years of relations they cut within seconds, they are not social person, they are not diplomats.

They see various ups and downs in their life and till the middle age their life is full with trials and experiences. They are very rich in many experiences but lag behind socially. They never look back; they are very optimistic and go ahead soon. The second half of their life is completely a changed life. They have knowledge of various arts and subjects; they learn from their trials, their experience is vast, which many people do not have.

The energy of the nakshatra favors cutting and burning for creation. Cooking is one such activity where both are required. Hence, they take great interest in cooking activities. This nakshatra has strong connection with source of energy and power, and it deals with fire and metabolism in our body. So, many Krittika people work with fire related jobs.

The nature of the nakshatra is sharp and soft. The process of cooking requires softness with the heat of fire otherwise food will burn. They are soft in nature but often burn their outcome or food, because they lack patience. The food looks delicious when it is hot but we have to eat it with caution. Hence, Krittika natives look very smart and charming but inside a razor-sharp person are sitting and the heat is not an ordinary heat, it is excessive and fierce. Krittika people always like to eat hot food and they can drink a hot cup of tea very fast.

When they find anything wrong or untruthful or someone take undue advantage of their soft behavior, then immediately a sharp knife come out. They are ready to cut immediately everything and burn it forever. Their move is totally unexpected and surprises others but they are not negotiators. When they leave anything, they leave it forever. There are no negotiations with fire only it has to calm down by removing fuels.

Fire is sharp and also provides comfort; it is both friend and enemy. An uncontrolled fire is dangerous, but when it is controlled, it works as a friend; it cooks our food, and makes us warm. A small quantity of fire we require in everyday of our life, without which everything would become freeze.

Fire is necessary to create something, and the Sun is the creator of the everything that exists on the universe. So, this nakshatra has strong connection with creation. Krittika people are very creative and always produce innovative ideas. As strong fire is required to create something big, they have capacity to create something big and often use the term; big, large, great, broad, tremendous in their discussions.

They are very liberal and broad-minded person. They are very good advisors. They always think about an aim or a purpose or how to penetrate a difficult task. They do deep enquiry and easily identify the cause of imperfection. Their eyes are like scanners, who can easily detect anything wrong in the piles of luggage. Hence, they always look for perfection and not ready to accept anything below the quality. Their vision is very deep and they have a strong mind which does not satisfy by only superficial observations. They are deep thinkers and have ability to see the root cause of the problem.

According to science, when the oxygen in the air combines with the carbon and hydrogen in the fuel, a chemical reaction occurs. In this process energy is released in the form of heat and light, which is called fire. Fire burns everything and never shows any mercy. To play with fire is very dangerous as it can create serious harm on a slight mistake. Hence, it is not good to play with Krittika people, their hidden fire can burn anytime when necessary chemical reaction takes place.

A very soft person can convert into a very fiery person, a big danger exists on the next level, and the chain reaction begins with no time. Following are some points that describe the quality of fire and the characteristics of Krittika people;

1. Fire sparks suddenly, so they are blunt.

2. Fire provides protection, so they are protective.

3. Fire provides strength and support; they are ready to provide strength and support.

4. Fire provides light and the way out from darkness, they always provide proper and valuable guidance to others.

5. Fire provides warmth and care, so other people feel comfortable in their vicinity.

6. Fire is sharp, so, their logics and reasoning are very sharp and penetrating.

7. Fire creates a distance; therefore, they always maintain a distance and are unable to come to close to anyone.

8. Fire creates isolation, so they are lonely people and keep friendship with very few people.

When the process of burning starts it is difficult to control till the fuel exist, in the same way, Krittika people do not listen to anyone. Fire has the property of burning everything around it, similarly if they are doing one thing and they find something similar nearby, they want to finish (burn) it too. They finish it half, leave in between and want to complete another task (another burn). As fuel (motivation) is high, their process (involvement) is also high; when fuel runs out (no motivation) they drop it immediately and never regret doing so. Fire never repents, fire has no tears, it is the quality of fire to burn.

Fire indicates purity and thirst for knowledge. They are very honest person and always thirsty for knowledge. For knowledge they can travel anywhere and they keep on learning always something new in life. Having wide knowledge on multiple subjects they become good trainer, master and spiritual person.

They are very hard working and focused person. Being aggressive and adventurous in nature, they like to travel farther places and like to travel alone. They do not hesitate to accept any job which is far away from their native place. They are always ready to help others but never accept any help from others, if taken then they try to return it soon.

The puranic story of Karttikeya says that the six wives of saptirishis brought up the little boy and taught him various subjects. Hence, Krittika people are very close to their mother or any other woman like mother. They are multi-talented person but never show their ego. In many cases, those born in Krittika Nakshatra are brought up by their mother with another woman.

The puranic story states that the six-year-old Kartikeya killed the invincible demon Tarakasura, which tells us that the Krittika people have the ability to accomplish a difficult task with minimal resources. They do heroic deeds and never give up in any difficult situation.

On higher aspects, the constant burning fire indicates they are the seekers of the truth. This energy has strong power to penetrate the hidden chakras in the human body. They can become great mystics, philosophers and have ability to provide guidance to the masses. Their blunt behaviour can transform into a wise person who has ability to speak on various topics and instantly provide answer on various complex questions.

Negative Traits: The fire element produces a short-tempered person who can provoke easily and take any sharp object in his hand. Although they calm down quickly such behavior in front of others makes them unpopular. They are very straightforward and a non-diplomatic person. Their blunt behavior makes them unacceptable people. They never listen to the advice of others and often burn their fingers. They prefer to go alone and lack the spirit of teamwork which makes them misfits in the social circle.

They like to enjoy their penetrating power and to say stinging words to others. Instead of protecting others, they misuse the power of fire and prefer to burn others. These are criminals who like to insert sharp objects into the body of others. They are unfit to live in society and live near a cremation ground or any other place where the fire burns continuously. When a person is unable to control such fiery energy, he indulges in illicit relations and finds it an easy way to calm down his energy.

12.2 Uttara Phalguni

Uttara Phalguni is the 12th of 27 Nakshatras and is located at 26° 402 Leo - 10° 002 Virgo. The word Uttara means next, latter, subsequent, and remaining. It also means north direction, higher, superior, and excellent. The stars in this nakshatra constitute the remaining part of the Phalguni nakshatra. Another meaning of the nakshatra is "The latter red one".

Symbol: The symbol of the nakshatra is "Rear legs of the bed". When a person completes rest on the bed, it is his legs that provide the support to get out of bed and get back to work. Hence Uttara Phalguni people do not take initiative to fulfill their desires, they believe in doing hard work and maintain patience.

"A full-grown fig tree" is also associated with this Nakshatra, indicating that this energy bestows the fruits of one's hard work.

The difference between the back leg of funeral cot of Uttara Bhadrapada nakshatra, and the back leg of bed of Uttara Phalguni nakshatra is; The funeral cot people carry from one place to another place but bed remains at the same place. So, behaviour of Uttara Phalguni people are very stubborn and they don't like to change their decisions. They are very laborious person and have strong ability to sit at one place for long hours.

Caste: The caste assigned to the Nakshatra is "Kshatriya" (warrior).

1. Warriors are those whose ultimate aim is to win the battle. They don't settle for less than victory.

2. Warriors are belligerent, they have a strong ability to survive in difficult times. Once decided a warrior never deviate from the chosen path.

3. Warriors are ready to bear any pain to achieve the objective, mission is always important to them.

4. Warriors are totally dedicated towards their goal, they never retrace their steps and find their own way to continue their journey towards achievement of the goal.

Characteristics: Uttara Phalguni first pada begins in Leo and the remaining three padas fall in Virgo. The lordship of the Sun indicates creation and the lordship of Mercury indicates intelligence. Uttara Phalguni people use their intelligence in creative works. These people are very good in making unions and friendships. The first part (Purva Phalguni) indicates beginning of something and the last part (Uttara Phalguni) indicates ending, conclusion or finalizing things. This indicates that the interference of Uttara Phalguni brings the dispute to the table of settlement; hence they work as a mediator.

Purva Phalguni gives birth to the creation and the energy of Uttara Phalguni shows that creation to the world. When a child takes birth (Purva Phalguni), it is the legs (Uttara Phalguni) that support it to walk. But without linkage with its predecessor star, Uttara Phalguni can't utilize its intellectuality. So, its first pada falls in Leo, and rest three falls in Virgo, here creation is related to intelligence.

Sun always moves in one direction and never retrograde. Sun has a deep effect on these people and they have many qualities of the Sun. Uttara Phalguni people prefer independence in life and work as an entrepreneur, counselor, or engage in some other independent profession. Sun also indicates government, so they work for the government.

They always take firm decisions and dislike the fickle behavior of others. They are very solid people and committed to their words. They don't give heed to gossip and they don't like to listen to hot and spicy news. They are dignified people and others respect their knowledge and wisdom. They work as a leader and they are an expert in their field.

Uttara Phalguni is called "The star of Patronage". These people are benevolent, compassionate, charitable, and helpful person. They have strong willpower and can cross any hurdle for the achievement of their goal. They dream big and don't like to waste their time and energy in any dispute. Their behavior is friendly but they are very stubborn in their decisions. They are self-dependent and don't prefer to take anyone's help to uplift their career.

Under the influence of this nakshatra, people are thirsty for knowledge and truth. They are ready to travel anywhere for attaining such knowledge. They prefer to live in luxury but they don't feel an attachment to material things. They do not demand for their comfort, they are down-to-earth people and adjust themselves as per the circumstances.

With the Uttara Phalguni person, the story of King Janaka giving a lamp to a monk and asking him to roam around his palace without extinguishing the lamp fits perfectly, as the monk asked how he could live as an ascetic in this luxurious palace. When the monk had gone around the palace, King Janaka asked what he had seen in the palace. The monk replied that he had not seen anything as his attention was always on the lamp. Janaka said that this is the way to live in a luxurious palace.

Uttara Phalguni means "The latter reddish one" and red is the color of Phalgun (Joy and Happiness). Red is the color of sweet and blue is salty. The word 'latter reddish' means these people will get the fruits of success after very hard work. There is "No rose without thorns", this proverb fits perfectly on these people.

They never get disheartened by difficulties and always believe in working hard in life. Their legs are always ready to complete the difficult task and they never show their back. They never run from the circumstances and never weep about the scarcity of resources. In any adverse situation, you find that these people never complain to anyone, they believe in doing their work and they find their own ways to complete the work. They are the perfect "Karma Yogi".

Lord Krishna says, "You have the right only in doing your work, not in its fruits. Because the result is in the hands of God. That's why it is not right to run away from karma, nor is it right to expect the fruits of karma". The great warrior of Mahabharata Arjuna was born on the Uttara Phalguni Nakshatra.

Without expectations of the fruits, Uttara Phalguni people believe in doing their work and one day the red color blossoms and the success of roses comes to their hands. Red indicates caution and when a thing takes time to convert into red it can happen only when a person put in effort. It is only possible with due consideration and the person keeps patience with their fruits. Such a person takes utmost care to complete the work and leave the rest in the hands of God. Uttara Phalguni indicates that the fruits will come when the person keeps patience.

Uttara Phalguni people are choosy in nature, they spend hours to select the best. They work on multiple options and chose the best which is suitable as per the circumstances. Without options, it is difficult for them to take a decision, either in the matter of clothes or work. Once they decided they remain firm on their decision. They have a collection of various unique things at their home and they like to collect those items which are rarely available. They can spot a diamond among pebbles and they rarely do any mistake in their selection.

Due to the influence of Mercury, they are intellectual and sharp-minded. They dare to walk the unknown path alone. They take a keen interest in exploration and love to use their mind to solve mysteries. They read books related to secret and occult knowledge and spend a lot of time-solving the mysteries of nature. They accumulate knowledge that has become obsolete over time.

They are warriors and show leadership ability. They always encourage their companions and participate in every activity that requires determination to win. On the higher aspects, when creative sexual energy begins to enter the chakras, its ultimate goal is to conquer the sex drive and reach the crown chakra. It is the path of a warrior and winning this battle is their ultimate aim.

Negative Traits: If it is afflicted, then they can become greedy for prosperity and can do anything for money. Money can become the only motivator for them and they make relationships only with those people by which they can satisfy their greed. They can be extremely stubborn and do not like to give any importance to another person's opinion. They can become an egoistic person and highly arrogant in behaviour. They are dogmatic people and always keep their voices up in a meeting. They can cheat others to satisfy their greed.

They always want multiple options and are unable to take a decision. They always remain in confusion, about what to decide and what to leave. They are unable to take any decisions and waste their time and energy. Their behaviour delays various important things but they are not bothered about trouble faced by others. They have a misconception that they always take the right decision. Sometimes, they are too picky and take wrong decisions for their selection. They indulge in making many relations, contracts, and associations and face many problems. They prefer to run away from the situation instead of facing the problem.

12.3 Uttara Ashadha

Uttara Ashadha is the 21st of 27 Nakshatras and is located at 26° 402 Sagittarius - 10° 002 Capricorn. The word Uttara means "Subsequent", "Rejoinder", or "Answer". It also means "High", "Excellent" or "Superior". It is the remaining part of Ashadha star and it has the same meaning "Invincible" or "Unconquerable". Hence, the word Uttara Ashadha means "Later Invincible", "Final Victory" or "The victory that is immortal".

Symbol: The tusk of an elephant is the main symbol of this asterism, like Purva Ashadha. It is always in pair, so many astrologers believe that the left tusk belongs to Purva Ashadha and the right tusk belongs to Uttara Ashadha. The elephant is associated with Lord Ganesha and his idol has a broken left tusk.

Purva Ashadha is a concentrated energy that works to achieve maximum output by rejuvenating and removing, Uttara Ashadha signifies ultimate victory and emphasizes completion, utilization, and attainment of the ultimate goal.

Caste: The caste of the nakshatra is 'Kshatriya' (Warrior). Warrior never hesitates to sacrifice their lives on the battlefield. It is their duty to obey orders and have only one goal - to win. They know very well how to play with dangerous weapons and always keep them under their control. Planets in Uttara Ashadha indicate that such a person has all the qualities of a warrior; they fight very fiercely till they win and wait for the right moment for each attack.

Characteristics: This nakshatra bestows the person with many qualities. The 10 Universal Gods indicates 10 major qualities of the person and their focus is always on achievement. With all the combined energy these people have the potential to achieve higher things in life. They are intelligent and truthful persons who work without any partiality. They are able to see all the pros and cons of a situation, they never get scared and never run away from reality. They are ambitious persons who hold senior administrative positions.

People of all the three Sun nakshatra are very dignified people. They are not flatterers who lose their esteem in order to gain something. They are very firm and determined person who boldly face any situation and take decisions. Uttara Ashadha person never take any conclusion in hurry and it come from after thinking all aspects, as it is related to 10 devas.

Both Ashadha nakshatra are highly influenced by the characteristics of elephant. Lord Ganesha got his head back in the form of an elephant's head. Getting back indicates this nakshatra has strong potential to bring back the lost things. When Lord Ganesha got his head back, Lord Shiva gave him the status of being foremost among the gods. He has become invincible, the giver of victory and the lord of wisdom. The word Uttara Ashadha means 'Later Victory' clearly signifies the above story, when such a person gets his power back he becomes invincible.

Lord Ganesha lost his first head because of his arrogance and only to obey his mother's command. To show his arrogance, he hurt many deities because of his immense power, such an arrogant head cannot be where Lord Shiva resides. So, Lord Shiva cut off that head and again attached it to the elephant's head.

This story has great significance with the Uttara Ashadha people. They have many qualities which make them far ahead of other people. But due to such qualities, ego also makes a home in their mind. That subtle arrogance may be invisible to others but it can't be invisible to God and without removing that arrogance such a person can't be victorious.

Without removing that egoistic head, Lord Ganesha could not become the first God and be worshiped by all. The head that ego has gone can't be the same head as earlier. The replacement of head indicates that earlier head with arrogance will never return, that has gone forever. By removing that subtle ego, he has now become entitled to become the 'First God'.

In the same way, without removing that arrogance, Uttara Ashadha person can't become a victorious person and this star is an ultimate victorious star. So, loss is necessary in their life to remove that arrogance, it is a part of lesson and they have to learn that and remove the arrogance of being supreme.

When that subtle ego is gone, such a person's qualities shine like a bright star and he is now loved by all, he has attained the position of ultimate victory. As Goddess

Parvati wanted her son back at any cost and became extremely angry, in the same way many people do not want to lose the Uttara Ashadha person, as they are priceless people. They provide all possible help to regain his power. Just like Lord Ganesha got back his head, such a person gets everything back and is respected by all. Uttara Ashadha is an unstoppable star who got a late victory, but now it will shine forever.

Lord Shiva is the presiding deity of Saturn. Uttara Ashadha first pada falls in Sagittarius and the next three pada falls in Capricorn, whose ruler is Saturn. The festival of Makar Sankranti is celebrated in India every year when the Sun enters the Capricorn sign. Before this day every festival closes a month before and people eagerly wait for the day of Makar Sankranti. It also means that when the people of Uttara Ashadha get their power back, they only bring happiness in people's lives. They are the leaders who show light in many lives like the Sun.

Such a person can regain his money, business or power after losing it once. He is a completely changed person without any ego and is loved by millions, and then his name becomes immortal because of his great deeds. Now, he has achieved that victory that is unconquerable.

Negative Traits: They are obstinate and oppressive person who want result at any cost do not bother about sufferings of others. They are highly disciplined individuals, but cannot tolerate any disobedience and give severe punishment. They follow strict rules and force others to follow the same. They are ruthless and keep everything and everyone in their grip and don't let anyone escape.

They make everything an issue in the organization, write useless e-mails and they have the answer for everything. They jump into conflict and drag minor matters into court cases and feel the joy of victory to suppress others. They are highly vindictive individuals, and are unable to tolerate any kind of harm or negative word.

They have superiority complex and when someone asks for some improvement, they retaliate very fiercely. The energy of regaining and reactivating works in a negative direction and such a person can reorganize terrorist, racist group or army to seek revenge. They have subtle arrogance of their wisdom and power; never accept their mistake and this is the reason of sorrows in their life.

Chapter 13

Ways to Strengthen Sun

A weak Sun in the horoscope indicates low self-confidence. The Sun is alone, never retrograde, and its gravity pulls the planets into its orbit. A weak Sun indicates that the person is unable to move forward alone and is always looking for dependence. Sun represents the authorities and weak Sun indicates that the person may face problem with the authorities, lack of support from the father or his relations with the father are not good or there may be absence of the father.

Such a person frustrates very easily and feel depressed, suffer from an inferiority complex, unable to digest the word "No". A weak Sun indicates problem in eyes, and bone-related problem. These people are less socialized, suffer from frequent headaches, always feel insecure and look for security first.

Remedies for the Sun:

1. Chant Aditya Hridaya Stotra

2. Chant Gyatri Mantra

3. Chant Chakshushopanishad for problems related to eyes

4. Take blessing from parents

5. Avoid meat and stick to a vegetarian meal

6. Never accept any gift for free of cost, except parents

7. Donate dark red colored clothes

8. Wear Ruby

9. Chant Surya Mantra –"Om Ghrini Suryay Namah"

10. Avoid eating salt on Sunday - In India, when people fast on Sunday, they stop eating salt. If a person in whose horoscope the Sun is weak eats too much salt, then bones become weak, baldness and other blood related diseases occur. Therefore, to strengthen the Sun, it is good to leave salt in the food on Sunday.

Bibliography

Brihat Jatak, Translation by Prof. P.S. Sastri, Rajan Publications, New Delhi

Jatak Parijat, Translation by V. Subramanya Sastri, Rajan Publications, New Delhi

Hora Sara, by Prithuyasas (Translation by R. Santhanam)

Fundamental Principals of Astrology, by Prof. K.S. Krishnamurti

Fundamentals of Vedic Astrology by Bepin Behari

Secrets of Predicting Dasa Results, Prof. (Dr.) Nimai Banerjee, Published by Bhagyalipi Publications, Cuttak

Sun – The Cosmic Powerhouse, Prash Trivedi & Vela, Sagar Publications, New Delhi

Earth's Sun<https://www.space.com/58-the-sun-formation-facts-and-characteristics.html> Accessed on 10th Sept 2023

Sun<https://www.britannica.com/place/Sun> Accessed on 10th Sept 2023

About The Author

Ajay Srivastava is the founder of lotuswisdom.in and holds 'Bachelor of Science' from Deen Dayal Upadhyay Gorakhpur University, Gorakhpur (UP) and 'Masters Programme in International Business' from PSG Institute of Management, Coimbatore (Tamil Nadu).

He has extensive experience in the capital market as a Lead Analyst, Investment Banker, Consultant, and Advisor in identifying investment opportunities and formulating strategies. In his career, he has written various research notes and has done in-depth research from a commercial and financing point of view in multiple deals. With diverse industry experience and wide understanding, he started imparting his knowledge in the industry since 2013.

He has deep knowledge of graphology and very much interested in analyzing a person by handwriting and has analyzed the handwriting of hundreds of persons in his life.

He is very much passionate to learn about astrology in deep and has completed 'Jyotirvid' and 'Jyotirvisharad' in

Astrology from Bharatiya Vidya Bhavan, Mumbai. His various research articles have been published in the renowned magazine "The Astrological eMagazine".

Email ID: ajay.srivastava@lotuswisdom.in

Web Site: http://www.lotuswisdom.in/

Books Written by the Author

1. Psychology and Investment

2. Vedic Astrology: The Light of Wisdom

3. Midlife Crisis: An Astrological Appraoch

4. Jupiter: The Planet of Fortune

5. The Joy of Creation and Success

6. The Light of Nakshatras

7. Sun: The Supreme Creator

8. Astrology & Predictions

9. Animal Symbols of Nakshatras

10. Astrology & Profession

11. Rahu & Ketu: The Invisible & Mysterious Planets

12. Planets and Human Life (Coming Soon)

Astrology Courses

1. Vedic Astrology for Beginners {Level – 1 (Basics)}

Module – 1: Basics of Astrology

Introduction; The Zodiac; Elements

Module – 2: Signs

Meaning of the Signs, Elements of the Signs, Qualities of the Signs, Odd and Even Signs, Sheershodaya & Prishtodaya Signs, Direction, Colors, Caste, Fruitful and Barren Signs, Masculine & Feminine Signs, Places, Other Major Qualities

Module – 3: Houses

Meaning of the 12 Houses, Types and Classifications of Houses

Module – 4: Planets

Planets and their Characteristics, Planetary Relationship, Exaltation, Debilitation & Mooltrikona, Natural Karakas, Karakas in Jaimini Astrology

Module – 5: Planets in Groups

Natural Benefic and Malefic Planets, Gender; Color; Caste; Guna and Places; Planet and Tastes; Nature of Planet; Elements; Metals; Age; Cloth and Height; Vegetable and Fruits; Physical Constituents and Tendency; Maturity Age of Planets; Planetary Aspects; Seasons; Hora

Module – 6: Planetary Strengths and Weaknesses

Strength of Planets based on its degrees, Direction; Direction Strength; Maran Karaka Sthana; Yog Karaka; Vargottam Planet; Shadabala

Module – 7: Retrograde and Combust Planet, Gandanta

2. <u>Vedic Astrology for Beginners {Level – 2 (Advanced)}</u>

Module 1: Vimshottari Dasha System

Nakshatra and Planetary Lordship, Change of Dasa and Results

Module 2: Basics of Nakshatra

Deity, Animal Symbol, Caste, Activity, Gana, Guna, Gender

Module 3: Important Yogas

Know the 30 most important astrological combinations

Module 4: Ashtakvarga

Interpretation of Ashtakvarga Table

Module 5: Transit of Planets and their impact

Understand the effect of transit of Jupiter, Saturn, Rahu-Ketu

Module 6: Planets and Profession

Identify the influence of the planet and the direction of profession

Module 7: Weak Planets and Remedies

Identify the signal of weak planets and useful remedies

Module 8: Key Steps to Chart Interpretation

Course Offerings:

- 30 hours of live sessions (Level 1 & Level 2)

- Learn various astrological concepts with practical examples

- Mode – Online Classes; Recordings available

3. <u>Nakshatra Course</u>

Knowledge of Nakshatra is very important in astrology, without it one cannot understand how energy works and what will be the result of the transit of planets. Do not limit yourself to the movement of planets, explore the world of Nakshatra and understand the hidden secrets.

What You'll Learn

• How the knowledge of Nakshatra helps to understand the characteristics and negative traits of the person

• Effect of transit of planets and time of activation

• Meaning of each symbol and its influence

• Influence of the associated animal on the personality of the person

• When to start a new venture and when not to go ahead

• Related Profession

• Understand each concept with logic

Course Offerings:

• 60 hours of live sessions

• Learn various astrological concepts with practical examples

• Mode - Online Classes, Recordings available

• Medium - English

Contact Us:

Mobile No.: +91 9867837184

Email ID: ajay.srivastava@lotuswisdom.in

Blog: https://lotuswisdomonline.blogspot.com/

4. A Course on Animal Symbols of Nakshatras

In the ancient scriptures, a total of 14 animals are related to the 27 nakshatras, and the behavior of every person is limited to these 14 animals. To understand the various merits and demerits of a person, it is necessary to understand the different characteristics of these animals.

How to Utilize Such Knowledge

• You will be surprised to know that these animals decide whom we form a relationship in our life.

• These animals determine our relationships with our friends, our spouse, our partners, our juniors and superiors.

• This knowledge helps to channelize your energy in pursuit of higher goals in life.

• The human mind is a very complex creation and it is difficult to say why a person behaves in a certain way and why his behavior changes. Knowledge of animal traits can provide proper guidance in this regard.

Course Offerings:

• 14 hours of live sessions

• Learn various astrological concepts with practical examples

• Mode - Online Classes; Recordings available

Sun:
The
Supreme
Creator
A Research Work on
Astrological Aspects of the Sun
Ajay Srivastava

The Light
of
Nakshatras
A Comprehensive Work to Explain the
Functioning of 27 Mystical Energies
Ajay Srivastava

Jupiter:
The
Planet of
Fortune
Ajay Srivastava

Vedic Astrology
The Light of Wisdom
Astrology for Beginners,
Learn the Language of Stars
Ajay Srivastava

PSYCHOLOGY
AND
INVESTMENT
The Art of Investing in Stocks with an
Explanation of Human Psychology
AJAY SRIVASTAVA

The Joy
of
Creation and Success
Ajay Srivastava

Midlife
Crisis: An
Astrological
Approach
Understand The Timing Of Crisis,
Learn How To Turn A Crisis Into An Opportunity
Ajay Srivastava

Astrology
&
Predictions
Ajay Srivastava

Animal Symbols
of
Nakshatras
Ajay Srivastava

Astrology
&
Profession
Astrological Principles Behind Career
Selection, Downfall and Resurrection
Ajay Srivastava

Rahu & Ketu
The Invisible and Mysterious Planets
An Extensive Research Work to Demystify
the Mystery of Lunar Nodes
Ajay Srivastava

<u>Notes</u>

<u>Notes</u>